Table of Co

AWS

The Ultimate Guide From Beginners To Advanced For The Amazon Web Services (2020 Edition)

THEO H. KING

Introduction

Cloud computing is a model that enables convenient on-demand network access to a shared pool configurable computing resources (e.g., networks, servers, storage, applications, and services). You can make provision of it rapidly with minimal management effort or service provider interaction. One of the main advantages of cloud computing is the possibility of replacing spent capital on up-front infrastructures with low variable costs, which scale with your business. With the Cloud, companies no longer need to plan and purchase servers and other IT infrastructures in weeks or months in advance. Instead, they can instantly launch hundreds or thousands of servers in minutes and get results faster too.

The Amazon Web Services platform (AWS)

Introduction

Very often in the course of history, the greatest technological and non-technological evolutions passed almost unnoticed, while revolutionizing, or rather evolving the simplest daily actions of millions of people. In fact, nowadays, reading your e-mail wherever you are, or uploading your own music library online to listen to it later from another device, or pay the mortgage comfortably from home, are simple actions and in the order of the day. Yet, until just a few years ago, these were not everyday gestures at all. What has partly happened and it's still happening in part is an evolution of traditional information technology. This is the great scope of change, which sees the Cloud, along with other phenomena, lead the ICT industry towards the so-called "Third Platform." It establishes, in fact, the entry into the "third era" after that of the mainframes and the second phase linked to the diffusion of PCs, databases, networks, and client-server environments, this is the renewal of the ICT sector that promises to expand radically the use of information technology, as leading to new and intelligent varieties of solutions. In practice, Cloud Computing technology allows you to use any type of document without needing hard disks and digital archives. The software, instead of being installed directly on their computers, resides on the net; that is in the Cloud, literally in the cloud

Different servers would decentralize the performance of The Amazon Web Services (AWS) and then become accessible via browser and applications from any device having connection. The advantages immediately catch the eye, and it range from being able to access our files, our photos, and our documents wherever we are and at any time, to be able to travel lighter without having to carry storage units with you or even the same computers. There are not even disadvantages. Two, above all is the need for a connection, which may not always be available, or the temporary unavailability of the servers on which our data is stored.

The target of this book is to give readers a complete guide from beginners to advance for Amazon web service: Amazon Web Services (AWS), trying to illustrate the advantages and disadvantages of this solution and proposing an example of configuring a virtual machine instance on the cloud.

CHAPTER 1

Independently Manage A Cloud Architecture Through Aws Services

Among several technology terms and themes, one of the most popular is cloud computing. Virtually everything we consume on the Internet, such as games, social networks, apps, file storage, videos, and music, are all made available through cloud services. Cloud computing is the on-demand delivery of computing power, database storage, applications, and other IT resources over the Internet. This is at pricing, based on usage.

Companies like AWS, Azure, and Google, makes this computing power available as services on the Internet. The Amazon Web Services (AWS) is one of the most adopted cloud platforms and most comprehensive in the world, offering hundreds of services. It has millions of clients, including startups, large corporations, and various government agencies.

Taking into consideration the many benefits we have from using cloud services and adding this to the need for software and project planning and development, using a cloud-computing platform such as AWS helps us greatly in deploying our designs and architecture, from making our front-end application available, such as backend, database usage, to monitoring complex environments. Some of the architectural models and types of services that AWS can deliver to us for the benefits include:

1. Infrastructure as a Service (IaaS)

This eliminates the need for investment, monitoring, and maintenance on local servers.

2. Platform as a Service (PaaS)

This allows us to develop software on a variety of technologies, even without the need for a local environment.

3. SaaS (Software as a Service)

This is the Architectural model most adopted when using cloud architecture. In this model, companies can use the above models and deliver their software as SaaS, facilitating their integrations, communications, and features.

When we have an application available on the internet, regardless of the Cloud Company or Servers we use, we have several concerns to deal with, as regarding Networking and Security. Some of them are:

1. How developers will access applications and what features and services each team member may or may not access
2. What addresses, ports, and access will be exposed for each of our applications?
3. How will we do the scalability, both to make new instances of our applications available, and to reduce that scale?

When we use AWS, many of these concerns cited above are no longer critical. This is because AWS facilitates the deployment of these security features, making it easy to use and deploy in both our applications and our architecture. Delivering software, deploying, and keeping applications to be always available are no longer a much-needed concern given the tools available today. There are several tools and services that help us perform a Continuous Integration and Continuous Delivery of our software without much of a headache. Best of all, keeping applications always available zero downtime, even at deploy time.

In addition to AWS's own services, for example, Code Deploy, Code Pipeline, Code Commit, and Codebuild, we can cite third-party tools that do these roles very well, such as Gitlab CI / CD, Github Actions, Codeship, Jenkins, among others.

The AWS SDK allows you to access the AWS services directly from the source code of your applications. Today, many different programming languages have their respective SDK available, among them are the JavaScript, Python, PHP,.NET, Ruby, Java, Go, Node.js, and C ++.

With the AWS SDK, you can authenticate users through Facebook, Google, or you can Login with Amazon using web identity federation, store application data in Amazon DynamoDB, and save user files to Amazon S3, for example. The AWS Command Line Interface is a tool for AWS terminal service management.

With it installed and configured (Access Key and Secret Key), you can control various AWS services via the command line in the terminal and even automate them using bash/shell scripts. We can use AWS CLI to connect to AWS S3 (file storage) and make managing objects easier.

We can upload and download multiple files with a single folder-level command, or we can turn on / off an application instance on AWS EC2 or scale containers on AWS ECS. The AWS IAM (Identity and Access Management) is a service that helps us to control access to resources safely AWS. We can use IAM to control who is authenticated (logged in) and authorized (has permissions) to use resources in the cloud environment. We can use IAM to manage users and access several permissions for team members, applications, or the process at which they communicate between these services.

The AWS Identity and Access Management (IAM) is a feature of your AWS account offered at no extra cost. It would only incur charges when other AWS services are accessed using IAM users. Amazon Virtual Private Cloud (VPC) allows us to run AWS capabilities on a virtual network that resembles a traditional network, but with the benefits of using AWS scalable infrastructure.

We can specify a range of IP addresses for the VPC, add subnet, join security groups, and configure route tables. The Amazon S3 (Simple Storage Service) is a storage service object that provides high scalability, data availability, security, and performance. We can use it to store any volume of data in a wide variety of use, such as websites, mobile apps, backup, and restore, archiving, business apps, IoT devices, and big data analytics. The Amazon ECS (Elastic Container Service) is a highly scalable, high-performance service for orchestration Dockers containers.

The Amazon ECS eliminates the need to install and operate its own software containers orchestration, manage, and scale a cluster of virtual machines or containers that set these virtual machines and is one of the AWS services when it comes to architecture. The Amazon ECS helps run applications microsserviços with native integration to AWS services and allows continuous pipeline integration and continuous deployment (CI / CD).

We can centralize legacy enterprise applications and easily move to Amazon ECS without having to make code changes. The Amazon CloudWatch is a monitoring service, task scheduling, and metrics. The CloudWatch collects data monitoring and operations in the form of logs, metrics, and events, and provides a unified view of resources, applications, and AWS services running on AWS. The CloudWatch provides data and incites

practical applications to monitor, respond to the system's performance changes, optimizing the use of resources, and get a unified view of operational integrity. We can also use CloudWatch to detect unusual behavior in environments, set alarms, view logs and metrics side by side, perform automated actions, troubleshoot, and discover insights to keep your applications healthier and less costly. The AWS Lambda allows code execution with no provision or manages servers. With AWS Lambda, we can run code for virtually any type of backend application or service without requiring server administration. Just load the code, and AWS Lambda takes care of all the items needed to execute and change the scalability of code with high availability.

We can set the code to fire automatically through other AWS services, call it directly using any mobile, or web application. The Amazon API Gateway is a managed service that allows developers to create, publish, maintain, monitor, and protect APIs on any scale with ease. You can create REST APIs to act as a "gateway" for your applications to access data, business logic, or functionality in backend services, such as workloads running on Amazon EC2, code running on AWS Lambda, any web app, or real-time communication apps.

Amazon Relational Database Service (RDS) gives an easy setup, scale, and operate relational databases in the cloud. The service offers cost-effective, scalable capability, and automates time-consuming administration tasks, such as hardware provisioning, database configuration, patching, and backups.

The Amazon RDS is available in various types of the database instance, with optimization for memory, performance or O. / I. Among the databases available, we have Amazon Aurora, PostgreSQL, MySQL, MariaDB, Oracle Database, and SQL Server. You can use AWS Database Migration Service to migrate easily or replicate existing databases to Amazon RDS. The Amazon Route 53 is a DNS service (Domain Name System), it is highly available, and it's a scalable cloud.

The design gives developers and businesses a highly reliable and cost-effective way to direct access to Internet applications by converting domains like The Amazon Route 53, which connects user requests, and the efficiency with infrastructure run on AWS are instances of Amazon EC2, Elastic Load Balancer, Load Balancing, or Amazon S3 buckets. We can also use Amazon Route 53 to configure DNS health checks and route traffic to endpoints, or to monitor the health of an application and its endpoints.

Above, we have listed AWS Core Services so that we can implement our AWS Architecture, even though we have several Front End, Back End, APIs, Databases, and other applications.

With the AWS Services listed above, we are able to develop, deploy, and scale our applications easily.

Accessing the Amazon system is very simple, especially if you already have an online shop account. By connecting to the Amazon Web Service portal, you can register your account without any fees; the process requires the usual contact information and a credit card number, including a prepaid one, on which it will only charge for consumption. Now, however, we don't have to worry about costs. Amazon, in fact, offers an interesting opportunity: it allows you to create virtual servers for low computational profile completely free for a year. This allows everyone to experience its potential easily before any massive use.

Once connected, we will have access to the AWS Management Console, where you can check all the services available on the platform. Here we will focus on the cloud computing system, called Elastic Compute Cloud (EC2), which you can access via the tab in the administration console

The EC2 cloud computing system represents, together with the S3 storage service, one of the most popular AWS products. The basis of EC2 is currently on seven data centers, distributed throughout the world in the USA (Virginia, Oregon, and California), Ireland, Singapore, Tokyo, and Brazil. The geographical distribution allows each user to decide independently where to use the calculation resources, considering any external requirements. The costs of using the various data centers are independent of each other, but, in fact, they are almost identical to all data centers with the exclusion of the one in Virginia that remains the most economical. By accessing the page showing the costs of use or EC2 Pricing, you can immediately notice the first big difference between a cloud system and a classic remote server: the costs are for hourly use, not monthly / yearly! This means that we can use a server for a couple of hours and then terminate it, only incurring the costs of the time we actually used it.

We can mainly determine the hourly cost by the desired virtual machine profile in Amazon instance as already anticipated, and the offer varies from the home server to the cluster for the scientific calculation. Obviously, the virtualization of resources does not require a definitive choice of the profile, leaving the possibility of varying it according to the needs of one's own instance, in reality, it is necessary to define a new instance, supported by the same virtual disks, but the result would be the same.

Combining these two features, we obtain the interesting ability to create dynamic systems that automatically scale the number of resources used, optimizing the efficiency/cost ratio.

MICRO INSTANCES AND FREE TIERS

In these examples, we will use an instance of the micro profile; micro instances (t1.micro code) provides a limited amount of computing resources, which can be increased for short burst periods when the underlying infrastructure is unloaded.

The micro profile is suitable for low load applications, small websites, or to test your installation before making it public through a more performing profile. An instance of this type currently includes:

- 2x EC2 CPU (available for short-term bursts)
- 613 MB RAM
- Storage on EBS

Before continuing, let's clarify a little the terminology in use. Being a service, based on virtualization, Amazon had to define its own metric and nomenclature for the resources made available to the instances. The most important concepts are the EC2 CPU and EBS:

EC2 CPU is the abstraction for the processor; the basis of Amazon's hardware infrastructure is currently on Intel Xeon and AMD Opteron processors of different models and capacities. To offer a service comparable to each user, the CPU performance is abstracted in the concept of EC2 CPU whose frequency values are decided arbitrarily and variable over time by Amazon itself;

Elastic Block Storage (EBS) is one of the two different types of mass memory abstractions, usable on Amazon to define virtual disks. EBS relies on the S3 storage service and provides a persistent and durable memory with restarts and terminations of the instances (with the necessary precautions); the alternative is called storage instance, and this represents a low-cost mass memory but with the characteristic of not being persistent when a request is restarted. Usually, an EBS disk is preferred for all static data operating system software. While we can use the other storage for temporary contents, or durability not required.

Using a micro instance in testing or pre-production, has a significant advantage when you begin to examine usage costs; in fact, through the Free Tier promotional system, it is possible to use a micro 7 / 24h instance completely free of charge for a whole year within certain traffic limits and using EBS. This is an excellent opportunity to try out various Amazon technologies and services and their potential for integration with EC2.

The First Instance

Let's go to the EC2 dashboard and get ready to run our first instance. Once you have chosen the data center region in the left panel, press the Launch Instance button, AWS - EC2 management dashboard. The system uses a very simple and intuitive wizard: we move forward after selecting "Classic Wizard."

EC2 Setup - Wizard

At this point, we must tell EC2 which operating system to install; on the AWS platform, we actually talk more properly about AMI, an acronym for Amazon Machine Image. An AMI represents a virtual machine used as a template basically, with any operating system pre-installed and ready to be used on the virtualization environment prepared by Amazon itself. An AMI can represent both a "virgin" operating system, which is a mere basic installation without additional configurations, and it's a system already equipped with the most varied services of common use (e.g., Web, DBMS, FTP, and Mail). The types of AMI present are many: we have paid, free, officially prepared by Amazon, created by members of the community. This typically meets the needs of most users. However, for sensitive systems, it is always a good idea to start from clean and released AMIs or from the official channel or from known companies participating in the community, in order to avoid finding a badly configured system, difficult to manage or, worse still, equipped with backdoors. In this guide, we selected a classic Ubuntu 12.04 LTS server, in the 64-bit version.

EC2 SETUP - AMI SELECTION

At this point, we must assign our request to a billing profile, so that its performance is established. At the same time, we must consider the operating costs charged by Amazon; considering that this is our test environment and that we will eventually be able to modify the profile later, we associate the instance with the Micro profile, free in the first year of registration.

EC2 SETUP - INSTANCE SELECTION

We can quickly get the next screen, which lets us select advanced details out of the scope of this guide. We can select only useful points, "Prevention against accidental termination" checkbox. Among the commands to manage an instance, we can distinguish these two immediately; these are the Stop and Termination. The first represents the normal shutdown request, which is activated when you press the power-off button on a modern computer, thus starting the ordered shutdown of the machine. The second is a termination request for which the system is not only forcibly turned off, avoiding the shutdown procedure, but all the data relating to the instance are deleted, both its configuration and the associated virtual disk. In essence, the termination is equivalent to the request for complete cancellation of an instance, and therefore, the flag set in this screen requests a double confirmation for this type of operation.

EC2 SETUP - INSTANCE DETAILS

The next step is fundamental and involves the creation of the pair of public/private keys to connect to the server via SSH with administrative rights root; we insert an identification string for our key pair and save the generated files in a safe place.

EC2 SETUP - CREATING SSH KEYS

The next step is to configure the onboard firewalls; in fact, Amazon's network architecture requires that the instances are never exposed directly on the network, but only accessible through Amazon firewalls through the NAT technique. At the moment, we are not interested in changing the configuration of the perimeter firewalls, so we leave the default setting that only allows SSH traffic (for the more paranoid it is possible to restrict access to specific IP sources right now).

EC2 SETUP - FIREWALL CONFIGURATION

We are now in the last step, the inevitable review screen, which is where our choices are shown, and we are asked to confirm or change the various settings. We confirm everything via the Launch button and prepare ourselves to access our first instance.

EC2 SETUP - SUMMARY

A few seconds to wait and our instance will appear on the main panel of the management console. In a few simple steps, our first virtual server is ready to take advantage of the potential of the Amazon cloud

NETWORK CONFIGURATION

ELASTIC IP

Amazon's perimeter routers allow you to communicate with your instance via a DNS name, like ec2-192-51-128-176.eu-west-1.compute.amazonaws.com; however, most of the time this is not desirable as we would like to use a public IP address for our instance, in order to associate our registered domain to it or simply for a more free management of the network port configuration. To this end, Amazon has a large number of public IP addresses, which are available to EC2 customers free of charge; these addresses, internally called Elastic IP (EIP), which you can request, associate, and release dynamically according to your need. Excluding some problems with the various CBL communities that we will examine later, this dynamic assignment policy allows us to associate a public IP to our instance immediately. In reality, the EC2 instance uses only private IPs, which Amazon's network defines it internally as the public IP and the private IP. The private IP association is delegated to the perimeter systems, which set up a NAT 1-1 between the two addresses; although in the rest of the guide, for simplicity, we will often refer to the public IP of the instance, remember that an EC2 instance has only private IP addresses subjected to NAT.

To associate an EIP to our instance, simply open the corresponding menu on the bottom right (Network & Security -> Elastic IPs) and click on the Allocate New Address button, as shown in the figure.

EIP ALLOCATION

The process is instantaneous, and we can immediately associate the address to the instance using the Associate Address button. As mentioned above, the EIP service is free for all EC2 customers; in reality, there is a limitation: the allocation of EIP is free for as long as they are associated with an instance, otherwise, if they are kept allocated but not associated, an hourly service fee is provided. Obviously, the marketing concept behind the offer is to encourage as much as possible the use of the EC2 architecture, allowing Amazon to attack the fixed costs, which are naturally enormous for a similar architecture.

We verify the successful association of the IP address to the instance by connecting us via SSH to our system:

SSH -imykey.pem root @ <EIP>

FIREWALLS AND BALANCERS

Amazon allows advanced network configurations through simple Web interfaces; this is the case, for example, of two of the most used network components within the Amazon platform: the firewall configuration system and the automatic load balancing system. Let's focus on configuring firewalls, and then briefly discuss the concept of balancer and its possible uses in combination with other Amazon tools.

A firewall, in its classic sense mostly, is a hardware/software system designed to control the flow of packets from one network to another. In particular, a firewall implements a set of rules that define open/closed ports with respect to network parameters such as, Source IP, destination IP, protocol (ICMP, UDP, TCP), source, or destination port. In EC2, the configuration of these systems is very agile, and we can verify it immediately by clicking on Security Groups, part of the NETWORK & SECURITY menu.

EC2 FIREWALL CONFIGURATION

A Security Group represents a set of firewall rules that can be associated with an arbitrary number of instances; vice versa, each instance must be associated with a single Security Group. This abstraction allows you to define firewall rules common to multiple instances, while at the same time ensuring the maximum possibility of customization for specific needs of a single instance.

We select the default Security Group and open the inbound drop-down menu; in this panel, we can define the firewall rules that we want to apply to the incoming ports. If you already have some firewall configuration practices, you will notice that it is not possible to set rules on outgoing ports, a limitation that can be circumvented by defining the aforementioned rules through a local firewall at your own instance e.g., via iptables. Considering our LAMPP architecture, we create new rules to allow access to each IP of ports 80 (HTTP) and 443 (HTTPS), setting the desired protocol (or "Custom TCP rule" if not present in the list) and the addresses in the white list (0.0.0.0/0 implies the whole network). We can refine the configuration a little by limiting access to ports 21 (FTP) and 22 (SSH) only to some IP addresses in order to make our location less vulnerable. Apply Rule Changes and verify that everything works as expected by loading the Apache test page, available at the IP address assigned to us in the previous paragraph.

To conclude the discussion on the main network-level features available on EC2, let us briefly discuss the balancing issue. An IP balancer is simply a device capable of distributing incoming traffic to multiple outputs very quickly and, conversely, of re-aggregating, the return flows to the original input. This allows you to scale rapidly network services subjected to high traffic, using standard servers without scaling the hardware to expensive high parallelism (super-computer) systems. In Amazon, the application of a balancer combined with the features of virtualized cloud hardware, enables innovative and dynamic balancing features. In fact, through user-definable rules, it is possible to realize a system whereby the EC2 instances are cloned and added to the balancer (and vice versa: removed and terminated) when the load exceeds/falls within certain thresholds. This allows, for example, to define a low-profile Web server, suitable for the load considered normal, which is not affected by slowing down or problems due to the momentary increase of the load (when a clone under the same balancer is created to reduce its work). Obviously, setting up a balancer requires a careful study of its software architecture as not all services can be cloned/destroyed without consequences (in general, only those that perform read-only operations are suitable). This allows, for example, in defining a low-profile Web server suitable for the load considered normal, which is not affected by slowing down the problems due to the momentary increase of the load when a cloned under the same balancer, created to reduce its work. Obviously, setting up a balancer requires a careful study of its software architecture as not all services can be cloned/destroyed without consequences; in general, only those that perform read-only operations are suitable. This allows, for example, defining a low-profile Web server, suitable for the load considered normal, which is not affected by slowdowns or problems due to the temporary increase in load when a clone under the same balancer is created to reduce its work. Obviously, setting up a balancer requires a careful study of its software architecture, as not all services can be cloned/destroyed without consequences; in general, only those that perform read-only operations are suitable.

SNAPSHOTS AND BACKUPS

We conclude this overview of the EC2 service by talking about the snapshot functionality available on EBS, how it can perform full backups by the server. A snapshot is a byte-byte copy of an EBS volume that, like the latter, is stored internally on the S3 storage service. The benefit of a snapshot is that it can quickly be converted into an EBS volume, making it possible to create full backups and fast recovery for the most critical servers.

SNAPSHOT OF AN EBS VOLUME ON EC2

This section allows you to manage all your snapshots; please note that being hosted on EBS, snapshots have a fixed cost per gigabyte. To create a new snapshot, select the "Create Snapshot" button at the top: select the volume whose snapshot you want to execute and insert some comments that allow you to identify it. Finally, confirm the operation using the "Create" button and wait for the copy to be completed. If your goal is to use the snapshot as a total server backup to restore it from scratch in the event of serious problems, we suggest creating the snapshot with the system turned off.

SNAPSHOT OF AN EBS VOLUME - VOLUME SELECTION

Once the copy is finished, you will have the snapshot available in the dedicated section. By selecting the snapshot, it is possible, for example, to create new EBS volumes, restoring the server status to the exact same conditions as when the snapshot was created, creating a fast and intuitive disaster recovery system if performed regularly. However, remember that for a better disaster recovery process, you can transfer snapshots to datacenters other than those where the instance is present. Currently, the EC2 web interface does not allow this operation, which can only be performed using external software. Finally, the snapshot can also be used to create your own AMI to have its own template for the creation of subsequent instances.

CHAPTER 2

Create A Computing Infrastructure Using Scalable Virtual Servers

When a website, like an online store, is at the center of your business, the site's ability to serve customers through traffic spikes and sudden server failures can mean the difference between a big win and a frustrating loss. Therefore, while setting up a single virtual server for work is simpler than ever, it is worth spending a few minutes considering a high availability cluster. In a cluster, rather than running everything on one machine, the different parts of the server architecture that you can manage by separate server instances. In this configuration, you can resize the server by adding more workers when the load increases and keep the server running even if one or more workers stop for any reason.

We would use ClusterCS and Amazon Web Services to create a scalable server cluster and use it to host a WordPress site for a WooCommerce-based e-commerce site.

1. Set up your ClusterCS account. ClusterCS represents a control panel for servers in the cloud. It brings the power of normal control panels to virtual and dedicated servers, collecting them all behind a single interface. The original creation of this tool was to manage hosting accounts managed by Soft Dreams; the company behind it, so it is was well tested in real production environments. ClusterCS supports multi-server applications such as the WordPress site optimized for e-commerce that we will develop in this tutorial, in addition to maintaining personal servers. In order to get started, you should visit the ClusterCS website and create an account. A free account allows you to manage a single server and up to five separate domains running on it. A cluster configuration divided over multiple servers requires a paid account, but many of the steps you will see in the tutorial are also applicable to a single server configuration.
2. Begin some virtual servers in a cloud-based control panel, ClusterCS works with any virtual or dedicated server: you can use it to control servers on Digital Ocean, AmazonWeb Services (AWS), or even on a

virtual machine running on your laptop.

We will use the AWS. If you currently don't have an AWS account yet, you can sign easily up for an account. Then, log in to the AWS Console to create server instances for installing our website.

The configuration we will create is as follows:

- Load Balancer (libbre): This instance will be the outside of the cluster. It will also keep your website files.
- Minimum of two application servers (app1 and app2): The instances are responsible for running the web. Having more than one application server gives the configuration more resilient, if one goes down, the others can still serve the application pages. Furthermore, adding multiple application servers is a quick way to respond to increased traffic.
- Database server (DBs): Having the database aside from the app servers adds a level of security while making the database available to all the servers that uses it.

We run the servers!

Step 1: Create a security group

When starting servers for a cluster, it is important to make sure they can communicate with each other and that ClusterCS can reach them using SSH.

On Amazon Web Services, you can perform the firewall configuration by using a security group. We will create one at the beginning, but if you have connection problems at any time, you can always go back to checking and changing the settings.

In the left menu of the AWS EC2 Administration Console, click on Security Groups. Then click on Create a security group.

When you get a pop-up sound, it requests you to give your security group a name and a description. Then, click on; Add rule add new rules one by one.

Firstly, allow SSH access from the ClusterCS IP addresses

193.226.133.91/32 and

85.9.60.46/32

Then, allow HTTP and HTTPS access (ports 80e 443)

From all the available options so that your customers can access your website. At this point, the security group configuration will look like this:

Click Create to save changes.

After creating the security group, it has an ID, which you can use to configure access between cluster server instances.

In the security list groups, select the new one you created and open the Incoming tab. You will see the rules you have just created. Copy the security group ID (a string starting with sg-) and click the change button to change the rules.

Add a new rule with the security group ID as the traffic source. You can choose to allow all TCP traffic from this source or, if you prefer to be more specific, you can use the following list of ports: 25, 80, 110, 111, 143, 443, 465, 587, 993, 995, 2049, 892, 32803, 21, 2049, 111, 892, 662, 32769, 8080, 8081, and 8082.

At this point, the configuration will look like this: To be able to connect to AWS instances from your computer, add an SSH rule for your IP. There is an option ("My IP") on the AWS, so it is not necessary to search for your IP.

Finally, to allow FTP access to upload files to the server cluster, add ports 21 and 50500

Once done, you are ready to start some servers.

Step 2: Start four instances of the ECS AWS server

With the security group in place, it's time to start AWS instances for the cluster. AWS offers many options for customizing virtual servers, but most of the time, the default options are a good choice.

Return to the EC2 dashboard and click Start Button Instance.

Clicking the button starts a seven-step guided procedure for starting the server.

In step 1, you can select the base image for your virtual server. Choose the first option, Amazon Linux AMI, by clicking the Select button after it.

In step 2, choose the instance type that fits the needs of your website; a smaller instance will not be able to handle as much traffic as a larger one, but a larger one will be more expensive. Consider the roles that the machines will play in your cluster. For example, you can add new application servers in response to an increased load on the server, but adding database resources is much more difficult. That's why it's better to run the database on a bigger server with more memory, than the app servers are.

In steps 3 to 5 of the startup wizard, go through the options to see if there is something you want to change, but most likely, the default options will be useful for configuration.

In step 6, select the "Select an existing security group option," and select the security group we defined earlier.

Finally, check your settings and click "Launch" to begin the necessary instances.

During this last step, AWS will request you to specify and later download an SSH key pair to access the servers.

Choose to create a new key pair option and enter a descriptive name for the key pair, then click Download the key pair to download the private key file.

Keep the key in a safe place on your computer. I like to put all my SSH keys in the

~ /.SSH directory, but you can choose any location."~" this means root base location. You can easily direct yours to any location of your choice

Once you download the key, the Launch Instances button will become clickable. You should then click on it and wait a few minutes for the instances to start.

If you are starting instances one at a time, repeat the procedure for subsequent instances until all four servers in the cluster are running.

Step 3: Link the elastic IP addresses to the instances

AWS assigns IP addresses to your instances upon startup. Stopping an instance releases its IP address. Since ClusterCS relies on the IP addresses of the server to connect to them, this can create problems if, for any reason, it is necessary to restart the instances.

To overcome this problem, you can use the AWS's Elastic IP Addresses options.

An elastic IP address is a fixed IP address that can be attached to any instance of the server. By using this address in the ClusterCS configuration, it is possible to keep it pointing at the instance even if you stop the instance.

Click on elastic IPs in the left menu of the AWS Console, and then click on Assign new button address.

Select VPC as Purpose, and click assign. It will assign an IP address immediately for use, then right-click on the IP address and select Associated Address to connect the IP to an instance of the EC2 server.

Click on the Example text field then select an instance from a drop-down menu that shows all your instances. Finally, click Member. Do this process for the rest of your EC2 instances.

Now you can access the servers using your elastic IP address, even after you restart it.

Step 4: Verify server access

Once the EC2 instances are up and running before switching to ClusterCS, you should check that you could connect to them.

First, change the permissions of the SSH key:

CHMOD 400 ~ /.SSH / key_name.pem

Then, look for the public IP address of the instance (IPv4 public IP) From the EC2 dashboard: Connect to it, for example using the command-line client (or PuTTY if you are using Windows):

SSH -I ~ /.SSH / tutorial-clustercs.pem ec2-user@54.162.85.168

In the event of connection problems, return to the security group settings and make sure all the ports that are required are accessible.

When you connect to the server, you should be ready to switch to ClusterCS in order to configure the server software on your cluster.

3. Set up the server cluster

Server instances are now up and running. It's time to set them up to play their part in running your e-commerce website as part of the multi-server cluster. You can do this by using the ClusterCS control panel.

The ClusterCS administrator is divided into two parts, which are the servers and domains.

The Server section defines the underlying system: the server configuration and the software running on one or more of the machines that make it up. The Domains part, which we will examine shortly, specifies the accounts and customer sites that runs at the top of the low-level configuration.

1: Add server instances to the cluster

Click on the Manage server to start configuring the cluster. If you use the free version, you will not be able to create a cluster, but the steps in configuring a single server are very similar to what we will do here.

Click on the cluster.

On the next page, scroll down to Add new server section. Then, you'll see some instructions, followed by a module.

In order to add the first server to the cluster, fill out the form with:

Server IP is the public IP address of the server. You probably would find it from the EC2 Dashboard.

SSH, port 22

User:

Ec2-utente

Access type: SSH key

Hostname: A name that makes it easy to keep track of what the machine does. You can use this field only as an identifier, so you can use any name you like, for example, Libre for load balancing, and the app1 the first application server and so on.

Now when the "SSH key" is chosen as the access type, a text area is displayed for entering the SSH key. Copy the contents of the

.PEM

These are files downloaded from AWS when you start the machines, and you can paste this into this text area. Leave the Key Password SSH field blank.

Once all the data are set, click on Next.

ClusterCS will then connect to the server and verify that it matches the configuration requirements. Once the check is finished, you will see the following results.

Click on Add server to the cluster pool.

You will see that the server has been added to the list of servers that make your cluster.

Scroll down, and then repeat the process for the remaining three servers.

Only then, click Continue with installation to configure the cluster and services you want to run on the different servers.

Step 2: Configure the cluster

Now that ClusterCS set all the servers for use, you can start the fun part of choosing the roles for each of the servers.

Assign a name to your configuration and choose a recipe, a model configuration you can use as a foundation for the configuration.

You can attach ClusterCS to an optimized starting point for PHP-based applications, called a Smart webserver (optimized LAMP). On a single machine where the entire configuration runs on a single server, this recipe is ready to be used immediately.

In a cluster configuration, you will need to do a little more configuration.

Click the customize command to open a detailed view. You will see the following list of "levels," combinations of software modules that together give the servers their capabilities. You can configure all the features of a level, create new levels, and add new applications to existing ones.

Start from the first level, Firewall by clicking on the Manage link next to its title. You will see the following view to specify the details of this level.

On the left side, you can pick the module that makes up the level (we will use the default set of modules, so you can leave that part in its initial setting).

On the right side, you can pick the servers that will execute this level. A firewall is something that every server in the cluster must-have. So select all four servers by clicking on their names.

Go through the rest of the levels in the cluster and create the following configuration:

Layer

Server

Firewall

Libber

DB

app1

app2

Smart Traffic Manager

Libber

Webserver

app1

app2

Database

Db

E-mail

Not used, remove from configuration

Webmail

Not used, remove from configuration

Storage

Libber

app1,

app2

Utility

app1

app2

We wouldn't add an email. If you want to use e-mail in the configuration, I suggest adding a separate server instance. This way, problems with your web server will not interfere with your e-mail or vice versa.

We have activated the storage level on the load-balancing machine and on the app servers. Subsequently, during the configuration of the site, we will select the libber server as the one that holds its files. You can mount the other two machines on NFS, so they will also have access to the data. This way, your website will not depend on any single app server, and you can freely scale it.

When everything looks fine, click Save to save the configuration and start the installation process on the servers.

Installation takes about 20 minutes, depending on the size of the cluster.

4. Configure the domain

A server cluster has now been created with a database server, two application servers, and a load balancing service that carefully routes traffic to different instances. We can start using the cluster by setting up a website to run it.

Click on domains in the ClusterCS main menu.

Click Add Domain.

Specify on this screen, how your domain uses the single server or cluster.

Domain name: You can configure the domain DNS settings outside of ClusterCS (point the domain to the public IP address of the load-balancing instance) or check the Enable DNS management option at the bottom of the screen and use the name; "servers of ClusterCS."

Username /Password: you will use the combination of username and password (or your customer) to access the site via FTP.

Access Type: this is the method you want to use (or allow your customers) to access the server.

Server

Server is the server or server cluster on which the domain will run. Choose the cluster you just created.

Storage location: This is the server where the site files will be stored. Choose the load balancing server (e.g., lb WooCommerce Cluster), as explained above.

Entry Point: the entry point is the instance of the server in the cluster through which traffic arrives on your website. This should point to the load-balancing instance that can drive traffic to the correct servers within the cluster.

IP: this is the public IP of the load balancing service

Note: When the configuration looks good, then click Insert command.

When the text displays "In progress," orange becomes "Active," then know that you are ready to use the domain. This step takes only a few minutes.

Optional: Configure Secured Shell Layer

On websites that handle sensitive customer information, such as people's credit card information, we recommend that you use SSL to encrypt the traffic between you and the server.

Using ClusterCS, SSL is easy to configure. In the Domains panel, click on SSL and you will see three different ways to configure SSL.

We will go with “Let's Encrypt,” a free and widely trusted certification authority supported by large organizations like Mozilla and created to accelerate the passage of the web to safe browsing.

Click “Install Let's Encrypt” to start the configuration.

Give the certificate a name, input your email address, and select the domain names you want to create certificates. Check the Automatic Renew checkbox, so you always have a valid SSL certificate.

Then click on the Start button, accept the displayed confirmation popup, and wait for the certificate generation to complete. When the certificate is set, you will see a screen with the information.

The “Let's Encrypt SSL certificate” is now set for use.

Configure the server cluster firewall to allow access to the load balancer from port 443, and your website is ready to accept HTTPS traffic.

On the dashboard server, besides your cluster, select Firewall. After that, scroll to the bottom of the page to add a new rule.

Set the new firewall rule using the following information:

Server: libber (the load balancing instance)

Protocol: any

Status: ANYTHING

Source IP: qualunque

(Source) Port Spectrum: All

IP destination: qualunque

(Destination) Port Spectrum: Exactly

Door: 443

Action: Allow

Active: Checked

Click the Insert key to add the configuration, and then on the Apply button to make changes in the server cluster.

5. Set WordPress

Now you are ready to configure WordPress. The beauty of this ClusterCS installation is that, even if you use multiple servers, the installation is no different from what you would do with a single server or shared hosting. So,

Step 1: Create a database for the e-commerce site

Start by creating the database. In the dashboard domains, select Databases, and then click "Add Database."

On the view of the next page, enter your preferred name for your database (for example,

WordPress) and click Create.

On the next page, you will notice that you have finally added your database.

You should then click on the “Add new” user button in order to create a new user.

When the installation requires you to choose the host from which the database user can connect the database, select any host. This will allow application servers to connect to the database, even if they are running on separate servers.

After adding the user, click “Member” next to the user's name to allow the user to access the database.

You will be able to choose permissions for the user in this database. Click on “Select all” to give the user full access to the database. Then, click the Associated User to implement the changes. You are set to use the database.

2. Install WordPress

Download the latest version of WordPress and use FTP with the username and password you used when creating a domain to upload it to your new site if your DNS settings connect to your domain's URL. You can also use the public IP address of the load-balancing instance.

When you have uploaded WordPress to your public html directory site, open the URL of the website in the browser and run the WordPress installation.

Use the following database information:

1. Database name: This is the name of the new database you just created.
2. Username: This is the name of the newly created database user.
3. Password: This represents the password selected for the database user.
4. Database Host: This is the private IP of the DB server instances. You will find this information in the AWS EC2 Dashboard. We use Private IP addresses for server-to-server communications within Amazon's virtual private cloud.

When the WordPress installation is ready, continue configuring WooCommerce and all the other plugins and themes you want to use on your e-commerce site.

So, come back for some final optimizations and learn how to resize your cluster up and down.

6. Use ClusterCS to optimize the WordPress installation

You have now set up a multi-server WordPress website on ClusterCS. The site is stable, secure, well organized, and easily scalable. However, what do you do exactly when your online store or other site receives a lot of traffic, and it's time to increase the service?

Step 1: Add the app servers

Here, you can see the power of a cluster configuration: thanks to work done in advance, when you need more processing power, it is sufficient to add more servers to the cluster.

First, start a new server instance on AWS, making sure it uses the same SSH key pair and belongs to the same security group as the other servers in the cluster.

Then, in ClusterCS Dashboard Server Management, click Manage to update your cluster preferences.

Scroll to the bottom and click Add Server.

Repeat the steps to add a server to the cluster pool from the top.

Click Continue with the installation and configure levels for the server. Select the same software as app1 and app2 Server. Then click Save to apply the changes. Wait until the configuration is complete.

At this stage, your website is running on three application servers, instead of two.

Step 2: caching

As simple as adding new servers to the cluster, it's not the only thing you can do to meet the growing server requirements. In Section Speed of the ClusterCS Domains panel, you can configure the guidelines for how to handle requests coming to your website.

As you used the "Smart webserver" guidelines to begin the cluster, you already have some optimizations in place: while PHP traffic is handled by Apache, there is a rule, "Static files on Lighttpd", which indicates to load balancing to route requests for static files like Lighttpd images to do some load on Apache.

CHAPTER 3

Create An Rds Environment With A High Availability Scalable Database

Amazon Web Services Today, we will see the Amazon RDS service for managing a relational database in a cloud computing environment. Cloud-aws.com Amazon RDS Hangout 18. Amazon Relational Database Service is a service that simplifies the implementation, management, and scalability of a relational database within the cloud computing that concerns AWS. Many applications uses a database that resides in the same machine as the application, this for a non-scalable environment that requires modest power can be fine, but if the conditions change, you need to use an external database through a service like Amazon RDS. CPU, Memory, and Storage are managed separately. Patches, malfunctions, and automatic recovery, Automatic backups, snapshots, and fast recovery, High availability with the primary and secondary instance, various engines such as MySQL, Microsoft, Oracle, etc. are Additional security via Amazon IAM.

Disadvantages

Latency, in fact, unlike a local database, network transmission must be added to the response time, but this, in a high-traffic environment with the need for scalability becomes a great advantage.

The basic structure of Amazon RDS is called DB instance, which consists of an isolated database environment. A database instance can contain multiple databases created by the user and can be accessed using the same tools and applications that are used with a stand-alone database instance. You can create and / or modify a database instance via a command line (Amazon CLI), using Amazon RDS's own APIs, or the classic AWS Management console interface. Each DB instance manages a different database engine. Currently, MySQL, PostgreSQL, Oracle, and Microsoft SQL Server are supported. Each database engine supports its own characteristics. Its instance class determines the memory and calculation capacity of an instance. You can select the class that best meets your needs, and if these should change over time, you can change it likewise. Obviously, the available classes have different prices that you can consult in the Amazon RDS costs section on the official website.

http: // aws.amazon. com/rds/pricing/

You can run a DB (database) instance in a virtual private cloud using Amazon's Virtual Private Cloud (VPC) service. When using a virtual private cloud, you can select the range of IP addresses, create subnets, routing, and access control lists. The basic features of Amazon RDS are the same in both a VPC and a non-VPC environment. There is no additional cost, for instance, in a VPC environment. A geographical region is divided into several zones, which are called availability zones. Each zone has been designed to work independently and independently, even if other areas suffer a breakdown. You can run multiple DB instances in different zones using the option called Multi-AZ. Amazon RDS creates and maintains a synchronous standby replica of a database instance in a different zone. A security group controls access to database instances allowing access to specific IP address ranges or EC2 instances. Amazon RDS uses three types of security groups: DB, VPC, and EC2.

In other words, the first controls access to DB instances that are not in a VPC, and the second controls access to DB instances that are inside a VPC, and the third controls access to an EC2 instance. Http: // docs.aws.amazon.com/AmazonRDS/latest/UserGuide/Overview. RDSSecurityGroups.html

It is possible to manage the configuration of a database engine using the DB Parameter Group, which contains the configuration parameters to be applied to one or more instances of the same type. If you do not specify this parameter group at the time of creating a database instance, the Amazon RDS service will apply a default DB Parameter Group value. When using Amazon RDS, you only pay for what you use, and there are no minimum configuration or activation fees. The invoice costs are based on the following criteria: Instance Class Running Time Storage Size I / O Request Backup Storage Data Transfer

Cloud Computing Amazon Web Service 1 Amazon Web Service 2 Amazon SNS Amazon MFA Amazon Free Trial Amazon CloudFront Amazon S3 Amazon Glacier Elastic Transcoder Storage Gateway Amazon SES Amazon CloudTrial Amazon CloudWatch Amazon SQS Amazon IAM

To do all this, we will use Amazon Relational Database Service (Amazon RDS). The service helps simplify the configuration, use, and scalability of a relational database in the cloud.

To get started, open the AWS Management Console and choose the RDS service in the Database list

Step 1: Create a MySQL database instance

We will use Amazon RDS to create a MySQL database instance. We have chosen the db.t2.micro class, and a 5GB of storage space and automatic backups, enabled for a one-day storage period.

A) Just at the top-right of the Amazon RDS console, select the Region where you want to create the DB instance.

Note: AWS cloud resources are hosted in data centers in different areas of the world. Each region contains multiple distinct locations called "Availability Zones" or AZ. You have the option to choose which Region to host your Amazon RDS activity.

b) Check the navigation menu on the left, click on Instances. Then choose the Launch DB Instance.

c) Choose the MySQL icon and click on Select.

d) The next panel gives you the options to choose your environment. Select MySQL under Dev / Test and click on the Next Step.

e) Now, you can configure your DB instance. In the list below, we show the example settings you can use for this tutorial.

Instance specifications:

License Model: select general-public-license, set by default to use the MySQL license agreement. MySQL has only one licensing model.

DB Engine Version: select the default MySQL version. Note that Amazon RDS supports multiple versions of MySQL in some regions.

DB Instance Class: select db.t2.micro - 1vCPU, 1 GIB RAM, equivalent to 1 GB of memory and 1vCPU.

Multi-AZ Deployment: For this tutorial, select No to create the DB instance in a single availability zone.

Storage Type: select the General Purpose (SSD).

Allocated Storage: type 5 to allocate 5GB of storage space for the database. You can scale up to 6TB with Amazon RDS for MySQL.

Settings:

DB Instance Modifier: enter a name for the DB instance; it is unique for your account in the selected region. In this tutorial, we will call it rds-mysql-10minTutorial.

Master Username: enter a user name that you will use to access the DB instance. In this example, we will use “masterUsername.”

Master Password: enter a password containing 8 to 41 characters (excluding /, ", and @).

Confirm Password: Retype the password.

Click on the Next step.

G. Your DB instance is now being created. Click on View Your DB Instance.

Note: depending on the DB instance class and the allocated storage, it may take several minutes to make the new DB instance available.

The new instance will appear in the DB instances list on the RDS console. This will be in creating state, until it is actually created and ready for use. The status available indicates that it will be possible to connect to a database on the DB instance.

Pending availability, you can switch freely to the next step.

Step 2: Download a SQL client

Once the database instance creation is complete, and its status is available, it will be possible to connect to a database on it using any standard SQL client.

a) In this step, we will take care of downloading MySQL Workbench, a very popular SQL client.

To download and install it, go to the Download MySQL Workbench page.

Note: Remember to use MySQL Workbench from the same device from which the DB instance was created. We can configure the security group in which you insert the DB to allow a connection only from the device from which the DB instance was created.

b) You will be asked to log in, register, or start the download. Select No thanks; just start my download to start the download quickly.

Step 3: Connect to the MySQL database

In this step, we will move on to connect the database created using MySQL Workbench.

a) Start the MySQL Workbench application and go to Database> Connect to Database (Ctrl + U) from the menu bar.

b) A dialog box will be displayed. Compile, as shown below:

Hostname: you can find your hostname on the Amazon RDS console. Port: the default value should be 3306.

Username: enter the username you created for the Amazon RDS database. In our example, it was "masterUsername."

Password: Click Store in Vault and enter the password you used when creating the Amazon RDS database.

Finally, click on, OK.

c) You are now connected to the database! On MySQL Workbench, you will see different schema objects available in the database, and you can start creating tables, inserting data, and executing queries and much more!

Step 4: Delete the database instance

It is good to delete instances that are not used, so they are not charged. You can easily delete the MySQL DB instance from the Amazon RDS console by following these two simple steps.

a) Return to your Amazon RDS console. Select Instance Actions and select delete from the menu.

b) You will be asked to create a final snapshot. For our example, select No in the menu, and check the confirmation box. Finally, click on Delete.

Note: it may take a few minutes to delete the database instance.

CHAPTER 4

Create A Private Network In The Cloud With Routes And Access Policies

Amazon Virtual Private Cloud (Amazon VPC) provides an isolated section in the Amazon Cloud, where you can run AWS resources in a virtual network defined by you. With this service, you have complete control over the virtual networking environment; in fact, you can choose a range of IP addresses, configure subnets, set routing rules, and configure network gateways.

This virtual network is very similar to the traditional networks that are managed within data centers, with the added advantage of being able to use the scalability of Amazon Web Services and connect their servers and/or applications directly with cloud services, using a high-speed network and without going through internet channel.

Network configuration in a VPC environment can be easily customized. For example, you can create a public subnet for web services, accessible directly from the internet and place back-end systems, such as databases and application servers, in a private subnet without internet access. In addition to the various network settings, it is also possible to manage various security levels, using security groups and ACL networks, to control access to EC2 instances.

Amazon VPC

For better security, it is also possible to create a VPN connection (Virtual Private Network) between your corporate network and the Amazon VPC network, which is in addition to ensuring a secure connection, allows us to exploit the AWS environment as an extension of our data center. With the same technique, we can also create a mixed environment, in which some servers are in the corporate network and others in the cloud.

Features

The functions and the possibilities of configuration in the VPC environment are very many, and as for other AWS services that we have presented, it will not be possible to see everything here. We will only list the most important features to find out more about new items.

Multiple connectivity options

In a VPC environment, there are several connectivity options, which allow us to connect a VPC network to the internet, to a data center, or to other VPC networks. All these are based on the AWS resources you want to make public or private. Here are some connectivity options:

Direct to the internet (public subnets)

It is possible to start an instance within a public subnet where it is possible to send and receive traffic from the internet.

Internet connection NAT (private subnets): you can use this for those instances that we do not want to be directly addressable from the internet. Instances in private subnet can access the internet without exposing their private IP address, through NAT in a public subnet.

Secure connection: all traffic generated from instances within a VPC can be routed to the data center via connections VPN on IPSEC.

Private connection to other VPCs: it is possible to connect different virtual networks owned by a single account or between different accounts.

Mixed connection: in addition, we can combine various connectivity methods to meet all the networking needs of your applications.

Security: Amazon VPC provides advanced security features such as security groups and ACL networks for controlling incoming and outgoing traffic at the level of instances and subnets. Optionally, it is also possible to choose to start instances on dedicated hardware in order to obtain an additional level of isolation.

Simplicity: you can create a VPC using the AWS console. You can select one of the network configurations that best fit your needs using the "Start VPC Wizard " button. In this case, the subnets, the IP address ranges, the routing tables, and the security groups are automatically created.

Example scenarios

We have seen that there are different types of connectivity, and by applying mixed techniques, it is possible to create many different configurations. Since it is difficult to see them all, we will try to analyze what are the most common:

(1) Public website: in a VPC network, it is possible to host a web application such as a blog or a simple website and to protect the site by creating group rules, to allow the webserver to respond only to HTTP and HTTPS requests arriving from the Internet, while prohibiting the webserver from starting outbound connections to the Internet. You can create a VPC of this type by selecting the entry in the console "VPC with a Single Public Subnet Only."

Amazon VPC

(2) Multi-tier applications: it is possible to use VPC to host these applications and enforce security restrictions between web servers, application servers, and databases. You can start the webserver in a public subnet during the application server and database in a private subnet. You can't access application and database servers directly, but can access the internet through a NAT instance, for example, to download patches. To create a VPC that supports this type of environment, select "VPC with Public and Private Subnets."

(3) Applications in AWS and Data Center: it is possible to create a VPC in which the instances of the web servers communicate with the internet and the instances of the server applications communicate with the database present in the company network. An IPSec VPN connection between the VPC network and the corporate network protects all communications between the cloud servers and the databases in your data center. We can create a VPC of this type with the option called "VPC with Public and Private Subnets and Hardware VPN Access."

(4) Extend the corporate network: you can move business applications to the cloud, start additional services, and add calculation capabilities by connecting a VPC network to the corporate network via VPN. To create a VPC that supports this type of environment, you can select "VPC with a Private Subnet Only and Hardware VPN Access."

Creation

To create the VPC, we need to go to the management console and select the Virtual Private Cloud service from the main menu. Once the VPC service has been selected, a dashboard will be presented, in which all the available resources and their operating status are listed. On the side sidebar, there are the entries concerning the service options, which can be used both before and after the creation of a new VPC. Later we will see a small overview of each item.

Amazon VPC

Now, to create a VPC, we must select the "Wizard" button in the dashboard and select the type of configuration we need. The options available are the same as those we have listed in the chapter (scenarios); if special things were needed, you could always change them later.

Amazon VPC

From this point, we select the scenario we need and enter the values that will be requested later. We will have to indicate a name for the new VPC, a range of IP addresses to assign to our network, define the subnets with availability zones, IP addresses, and the subnet name. Based on the selection, it is also possible to indicate the value of the NAT instance and the use of a DNS.

Main menu

This is the menu for configuring all the options in the VPC environment. This is present in the sidebar of the dashboard. The main sections are VPC, Security, and VPN connections. In the first, we find the options to modify the characteristics of the VPC, in the second, the security groups and the ACLs, and in the last section, we find all the parameters that concern the VPN connections.

Your VPCs: in this menu, you can view all the VPC configurations in the selected geographical region. We can configure new ones or delete existing ones using the options available on the screen.

Subnets: in this section, we can define the subnets we want to associate with a Virtual Private Cloud; the subnets can be private or public and contain routing tables, ACL networks and the definition of optional tags.

Route table: routing tables are used to route networks to the right destination; we can configure different tables and associate them with a subnet. This section must also be used to link two sub-networks together.

Internet gateway: in this section, we can configure gateways to be associated with the configuration of the VPC, which will allow the output on the internet to AWS components present in the subnet. The gateway must be associated with a routing table.

DHCP Options: here, we can modify the options concerning the DHCP function, which is used for the automatic assignment of IP addresses. We can define different DHCP options set, but only one can be associated with a VPC.

Elastic IP: as for the configuration on Amazon EC2, even in Amazon VPC, we can reserve statistical IP addresses to associate with our AWS resources. Remember that IP addresses are paid for even if they are not in use.

Network ACL: through this section, we can configure the checklists for accesses. On each list, we can define inbound and outbound rules and associate existing subnets. Optionally, it is also possible to define tags.

Security groups: for the configuration of security groups, the same list is used as in the Amazon EC2 service. In fact, even in a VPC environment, the groups must be associated with the EC2 instances that make up a subnet.

VPN Connections: in this menu, you can find all the options necessary to configure a VPN connection between the corporate network and the one in the cloud.

CHAPTER 5

General Knowledge To Incorporate Aws Technology Into Your Projects

Can you predict correctly the number of times you have heard of Serverless? I really have many, maybe too many, so I decided to use this chapter to give a practical overview of my journey into using the serverless service, as I was able to incorporate AWS in my projects after these processes:

IaaS (Infrastructure as a Service)

Do you know this server? Those strange computers in the dark rooms here are no longer fashionable... do you know why? It is because they are difficult to manage them. You need to use a thousand precautions, uninterruptible power supplies if the light goes away, the right temperature, absolutely no dust, fire doors, fire protection systems with argon and so on. So to guarantee a stable service without being mad and spend a lot of money, here is that services such as AWS, Azure, Google Cloud, and many others "rent" part of their data center, you just have to configure the infrastructure with a few clicks and worry only about the software part.

SaaS (Software as a Service)

After this great step forward, there are other problems (and of course, no one likes them). you need to keep the operating system installed on your virtual servers up to date, install security patches, configure scaling of computational resources, redundant the infrastructure so as to guarantee a high reliability of the service and everything, so what did cloud providers come up with to come to the contrary? Manage some of the services like MySQL, Elasticsearch, Redis, RabbitMQ, and many others, directly using the access without having to deal with installing and updating these services; obviously, the configuration (even if a little limited) is always possible.

FaaS (Function as a Service)

After this last step, there is still the problem of the virtual machines that will run your software (always the same problem as above), so what is the next step? The Serverless! That is managed platforms where the only thing you need to worry about is your code, nothing else, and it is the cloud provider that will automatically scale, update the operating systems that host your code, and guarantee its reliability.

NB: Server-less does not mean that there are no servers at all, but you don't manage them :)

Framework

After the initial study was done yesterday, today is the day of the practical test! Many guides explains how to create a simple API using AWS services, but the activation steps of the services are done directly from the web console, no matter how convenient, it does not allow you to reproduce the configuration steps easily, and the changes are not tracked. AWS provides a service called CloudFormation with which, by describing the infrastructure with a JSON or YAML file, you can provide all the resources you need in one go, manage updates, and rollback in the event of an error.

Of course, writing a huge JSON or YAML file is not very convenient, so I looked for which AWS frameworks it provides:

- SAM is a CloudFormation wrapper with extensive in-house testing capabilities, emulating cloud services.
- Mobile CLI a fairly old project, being phased out.
- Amplify the new and flamboyant framework for serverless applications.

I honestly found a bit of confusion about what to use, but the advice is SAM for API services, Mobile CLI to avoid, Amplify for more complex applications also with frontend. So I focused on the latter, to try the complete experience and see the news.

Amplify

This is very easy to use, maybe even too much. So just download the cli

npm install -g @aws-amplify/cli

Configure it following the guided steps

Amplify configure

Enter the main folder of your web application and add Amplify as a dependency

npm install—save aws-amplify

And as the last step, initialize the CloudFormation base stack where just a couple of access rules will be created and little else

Amplify init

Now comes the really fun part, adding the services our application needs, the Amplify CLI will always use guided steps to set them up. Taking an overview of what can be added, let's see:

- Analytics user behavior analysis system and various metrics
- Api to expose api and add the "server" logic -side
- Auth authentication, user management, login, registration, email confirmation, password reset
- Function simple functions with "server" logic -side
- Hosting services that will serve your application to clients
- Storage
- Services for saving, uploading and downloading files
- Notifications push notifications

Wow! There is practically everything and can be added with a simple command

Amplify add analytics

and once the selected service has been configured, deploy the changes

amplify push

Really nice, I already knew some services as Cognito for the management of utilities, S3 in combination with CloudFront to serve the frontend, Lambda for the application logic, API Gateway to make the APIs visible and in the end, DynamoDB to persist and save data.

Amplify is a great tool, especially for integrations with React, AngularJS, and Vue.js, that allow you to connect services quickly using your favorite framework. It took 15 about minutes to get a simple application (yes, the same old TODO list) up & running, but if you don't get your hands dirty putting them in the engine, I don't feel completely satisfied.

The integration

Authentication

I then begin to integrate my application written in Vue.js, starting from authentication. The configuration of Cognito is simplified a lot:

Amplify add auth

One minute and everything is set to manage utilities.

I was amazed at how many functions Cognito offers: confirmation of the email and/or phone number through a code (via SMS for the phone), log in with Google, Facebook, Amazon, and OpenID, up to serving you on a silver platter a complete server OAuth2. Creating this, from scratch, with a PHP or NodeJS server at least 1/2 days of work would have been useful; to think that it took us 1 minute is crazy.

Data

Now we come to the database, I had already used DynamoDB in the past for some integration, but never in combination with AppSync, a fairly recent service (it doesn't have more than one year and a half) that helps to manage access to your data using GraphQL endpoints. It should be said in the newest fashion!

With Amplify, it was really simple; you certainly need to have some experience with GraphQL.

Amplify add API

The answer to the command is clear:

? Please select from one of the mentioned services (Use arrow keys)

Ø GraphQL

REST

Not only GraphQL endpoints, but also REST! This is one-step ahead to pick the authentication method

? Please select one of the below-mentioned services GraphQL

? Choose the authorization type for the API (Use arrow keys)

? Provide API name: myNotesApi

Ø API key

Amazon Cognito User Pool

You can use either generated during this process, static keys, or go to use the authentication system created before with Cognito. Obviously, I choose the latter option.

The cold shower

Today I started writing the templates for my application. One of the most convenient features of Amplify is the automatic generation of GraphQL resolvers, even with transformers, to specify the access level. This last part is vital to limit user access to their data only and not to the entire DynamoDB table.

Here the first problem arose, I tried to follow the documentation faithfully but nothing, checking the generated resolvers I saw no difference using or not the @auth transformer. This took me a lot of time until, having surrendered, I created an issue on the Github repository to ask for support, they answered me really quickly, and it turned out that it wasn't actually working... okay, things that can happen.

DynamoDB

During debugging, I discovered that DynamoDB table indexes were created with Throughput Capacity for Reads and Write at 5, with no possibility of being modified.

For the uninitiated, this value is one of the parameters that are used to calculate the cost of the DynamoDB service: the number of reading or write accesses per second (it's not so simple but I don't go into the calculation). In order not to go into too much detail, this non-relational database answers for every query at the maximum possible speed regardless of the amount of data, and there is no limit to the number of rows (pay for the weight in GB of the table). The negative part is a somewhat difficult query engine, and we must carefully create the table indexes, which is vital for sorting and queries.

A difficult choice

Returning to us, I did not expect, therefore that for any test you would pay from $ 13 upwards of invoice, a little bit given that with less than $ 1 I have 2 IoT projects, an action of Google Home, my website (with two environments) and I use S3 to make an encrypted backup of some important files. With just 5/ 6 models, I arrived at disproportionate amounts, with a DynamoDB table ready for production when the application was not yet born. I, therefore, opened another issue, this time not yet taken into consideration.

I then deleted the project and got lost, I found a very easy to use and powerful tool, but it is still too young to be used. Being so simple, it does not even allow such a profound modification of some of its parts except with different workarounds.

Following several evenings spent evaluating alternatives.

A few days later, again

During the days, I collected several alternatives to Amplify; difficult to find because there are no other CLIs that with a couple of commands you could do ALL.

My choice, therefore, fell on the Serverless Framework, a very powerful and modular framework with a large community behind it that develops hundreds of plugins. I've used it previously for some cloud infrastructure and API automation projects, and I've always been satisfied.

Organize the project structure well

Resource management uses the CloudFormation templates directly, this ensures that it is always up-to-date and uses the features served by AWS without having to report the changes within the framework (an example is the Terraform, which uses its syntax, its integration to services, and can't keep up with updates and I've always found dozens of bugs).

When there are many resources to add out of those managed by Serverless, the official guide explains how to create them in the file. Don't make the mistake of putting everything in a single file of 2000 lines difficult to maintain, better to break it into more files

Resources:

- ${file (resources/cognito.yml)}
- ${file (resources/userRole.yml)}
- ${file (resources/queues.yml)}
- ${file (resources/tables/todos.yml)}
- ${file (resources/tables/projects.yml)}
- ${file (resources/tables/categories.yml)}
- ${file (resources/outputs.yml)}

And then, within these files specify the resources

Resources:

AccountTable:

Type: AWS:: DynamoDB::Table

Properties:

TableName: "${self: service}-${self: provider.stage}-${self: custom.todosTableName}"

AttributeDefinitions:

-

AttributeName: userId

AttributeType: S

-

AttributeName: id

AttributeType: S

KeySchema:

-

AttributeName: userId

KeyType: HASH

-

AttributeName: id

KeyType: RANGE

ProvisionedThroughput:

ReadCapacityUnits: 1

WriteCapacityUnits: 1

StreamSpecification:

StreamViewType: "NEW_AND_OLD_IMAGES"

This way, the code will be organized better and the files smaller and more maintainable.

Use a separate file for configurations

The previous discussion also applies to the configurations of the project, better to specify a separate file so that it can be changed depending on the environment or project without using hundreds of environment variables

Service: MyService

Custom: ${file (./config.yml)}

Provider:

Name: aws

Runtime: nodejs8.10

Stage: ${opt:stage,self:custom.env}

Region: ${self:custom.region}

The configuration file becomes much easier to view

env: "Stage."

Region: "eu-west-1"

TodosTableName: "Todos"

Simplify

Attracted by Amplify to use GraphQL, I immediately started using serverless-graphql, easy to use, and with a bit of organization and reuse of resolvers, I got to a good point. I realized, however, that I was really writing a lot of code, too; this meant keeping it, testing it, optimizing it, and taking away so much time in creating a simple CRUD functionality for the models.

API?

A doubt arose: do I really need graphQL APIs? Of course, they are really comfortable, expressive, and easy to keep up to date, but why do I really need it? More specifically: do I need APIs to consume? The APIs are mainly used to access the database, add server-side logic (which the user cannot manipulate), and make the service available to third-party services.

Access the data

DynamoDB has its own build-in functionality to limit access to rows, columns, and operations based on the user. That is; a user can only see certain attributes of the saved object (the "columns"), access only the objects that he has created (the "rows") and read some tables without the possibility of modifying them, all these are by identifying the user through Cognito authentication. What does it mean? It means that it has a security system for CRUD access already served without having to go through these code checks, it's already done! Is AWS to guarantee this security, do you think you are TU developer to do better than the team of 100 Amazon developers? You could, but in 99% of the cases, you'll be leaving out some vulnerabilities.

Everything can be said about the AWS ecosystem according to opinions, which is inconvenient, expensive, difficult, and complicated, but it cannot be said that it is not safe, so ok; I delegate this part to them.

Side note: once authenticated, a user with Cognito can access any AWS resource limiting access and operations through IAM Role. Not all resources support a granularity like DynamoDB, but only for file upload the S3 service can do it (think of the user avatar for example, comfortable!).

Server-side logic

Do I need it? What am I doing that I have to hide from the user? If I already know that he will only access his lines; at most, he is breaking the formatting of his data, well, he won't be able to visualize them correctly.

Surely eventually, there will be the need to call third-party services to add some features, so no problem with Serverless Framework. it's really easy to create Lambda functions where you can do whatever you want, the events that can trigger this custom logic are endless: from the creation or modification of an object in DynamoDB to the upload of a file on S3, even the entire flow of authentication/registration/ confirmation of Cognito users, nothing else is needed.

Service available to third parties

Need it already? Do we already have partners asking to take advantage of our services? If yes, you can create the entire API section that you want with Serverless (here the guide), creating only the endpoints you need; otherwise, you can skip this part.

API Gateway is an AWS service that allows you to organize API endpoints and manipulate parameters

So, API?

No, I don't need them now. I wanted to give Amplify another chance and use the client directly to log in to DynamoDB and use the AWS resources I need. It is very clean and very simple to use likewise.

In any case, for authentication to the API endpoint, one can use either Cognito (useful if they are called by the same application that serves the login) or the fixed keys and an access key generated by the OAuth2 endpoint served by Cognito. This last option makes the endpoint very professional by using the security of OAuth2 access and allows you to configure custom scopes to regulate access to resources.

The frontend

Once the backend sector is in place, the time has come to start creating the frontend part. I didn't have any doubts about the technology to use; having enough experience with Vue.js, I decided to choose this framework.

Thanks to the Vue CLI 3 the project, startup was immediate

Vue create myapp-frontend

and following the wizard, I chose a very simple configuration and then saved as a preset. The configuration to insert in the file.vuercin your user's home is

{

"PackageManager": "npm,"

```
"UseTaobaoRegistry": false,
"Presets": {
"vue-router-vuex": {
"UseConfigFiles": true,
"Plugins": {
"@vue/cli-plugin-babel": {},
"@vue/cli-plugin-pwa": {},
"@vue/cli-plugin-eslint": {
"Config": "base",
"LintOn": [
"Commit"
]
}
},
"Router": true,
"RouterHistoryMode": true,
"Vuex": true,
"cssPreprocessor": "stylus"
},
}
}
```

One thing catches the eye, why stylus? It was a choice driven by the component library that I wanted to use: Vuetify. I have already used it for some projects, and I have always found it good, I find it very complete for the number of components and, very importantly, it is very customizable.

Here too, thanks to the Vue CLI, a command was enough to add this library together with some example configurations

```
Vue add vuetify
```

Amplify JS

Having to amplify a management "à la carte" I directly installed what I needed as authentication

```
Npm install @aws-amplify/auth—save
```

Vuex

I wanted to use the Vuex module for a simple organizational; reason is to be able to manage access to data in DynamoDB through the Vuex state. I highly recommend it also, because if one day you wanted to change the access to the data totally, it would be enough to modify the state modules created for DynamoDB without having to touch the rest of the application.

Using Vuex module management, I created separate modules for authentication, data access, and credential management for AWS resources. As mentioned above, I used the same Amplify JS for a comfort factor, and it is not necessary to have the backend project to be used, it can be connected to resources also created with other frameworks or already existing.

I then created a Vuex module to manage access to the Amplify library and configure it

```
import Amplify, {Auth } from 'aws-amplify';
import AWS from 'aws-sdk';
export default function AmplifyStore(configuration) {
Amplify.configure({
Auth: {
identityPoolId: configuration.IdentityPoolId,
Region: configuration.Region,
userPoolId: configuration.UserPoolId,
userPoolWebClientId: configuration.ClientId,
mandatorySignIn: true
},
Analytics: {
Disabled: true,
}
});
Return {
namespaced: true,
state: {
auth: Auth,
aws: AWS,
configuration,
},
};
}
```

Amplify of his own does not expose the DynamoDB client so I had to authenticate the AWS SDK, so in a separate Vuex module I managed these clients outside of Amplify

```
import AWS from 'aws-sdk';
export default {
loadClients({ commit, rootState }) {
return new Promise((resolve, reject) => {
rootState.amplify.auth.currentCredentials()
.then (credentials => {
const docClient = new AWS.DynamoDB.DocumentClient({
apiVersion: '2012-08-10',
credentials: rootState.amplify.auth.essentialCredentials(credentials)
});
Commit ('setDynamoDBClient', docClient);
// more clients can be initialized here
resolve();
})
.catch(error => {
reject(error)
});
});
},
};
```

Now I can conveniently manage data access with specific separate Vue modules

```
//...
async getTodo({ commit, state, rootState }, todoId) {
const response = await rootState.aws.dynamoDB.get({ //rootState.aws is the AWS clients module
TableName: 'Prod-Todos',
Key: {
id: todoId,
userId: rootState.auth.user.id //rootState.auth is the Amplify auth wrapper
},
}).promise();
```

```
if (response.Item) {
commit('pushTodo', response.Item);
}
return response.Item; // return raw Todo object
},
//...
```

Webpack

However, I found a sore point, as of course there is aws-sdk: the AWS SDK for access to its resources. This package does not have modular API management, so installing it 35Mb is added to the node_modules, 2Mb compressed in gzip, which you will obviously need to serve to the client browser.

By completing the application, you will immediately notice the problem:

Webpack vendor chunk

We are talking about a 4Mb file of assets, unacceptable for having a light and fast frontend also using a CDN like CloudFront; in fact, the compilation tells us that it can use 4.5s with a fast 3G network.

Going to analyze what's in that chunk file, you immediately notice how much the AWS SDK (together with the PayPal SDK) affects.

Webpack vendor chunk analysis

I made some attempts separating the modules, but the result was the same, the solution I adopted has been configuring Webpack to break up files into many smaller chunks in order to take advantage of CloudFront's HTTP2 to serve asset files quickly.

I added the configuration splitChunksin the configuration filevue.config.js

```
module.exports = {
lintOnSave: false,
productionSourceMap: false,
configureWebpack: {
optimization: {
splitChunks: {
minSize: 10000,
maxSize: 250000,
}
}
```

}
}

Once again, the compilation was the result:

Webpack vendor chunk in multiple files

Many more files with very small dimensions and therefore much faster to download in parallel.

Deploy

Now, I developed the application by testing it locally, thanks to the functionality of the Vue CLI to serve, fill in the modified files on the spot, and reload the browser page when necessary. The next step is to make the application available to the whole world, since it is a static site that happens to be a bean for the Serverless ecosystem.

Pipeline

The AWS service in question is S3, it is simple to use, and it's with great performance; but what is needed is a pipeline that is unleashed when committing to the GIT repository with the task of compiling and copying the result inside the S3 bucket chosen to host the 'application.

Being a Gitlab user, I can easily create this procedure by adding the file.gitlab-ci.ymlwith this configuration to the project:

```
# Stages
stages:
- build
- deploy
# Configurations
Variables:
AWS_DEFAULT_REGION: 'eu-west-1'
AWS_BUCKET: 's3://my-bucket-name/'
# Build
build:
stage: build
image: node:8.10.0
cache:
key: "$CI_JOB_STAGE-stage"
paths:
- node_modules/
```

```
only:
- master
artifacts:
expire_in: 1 week
paths:
- dist/
script:
- npm install
- npm run build
deploy:
stage: deploy
image: fstab/aws-cli
only:
- master
dependencies:
- build
environment:
name: staging
url: https: // my-bucket-name.s3-website-eu-west-1.amazonaws. com/
script:
- aws s3 sync—acl public-read—delete./dist $AWS_BUCKET
```

It can be noted that the only building steps are the installation of NPM modules, NPM install, and then the launch of the npm script for compilation

NPM run build

This is simply what we are already doing locally.

The pipeline will be unleashed automatically as each commit on the master branch, as specified within each step

Only: - master Static website on S3

Now that we have the files compiled within our S3 bucket, this functionality must be enabled. To do this, just go to the AWS console, select the S3 service, select our bucket, select the Properties tab, and enable the Static website hosting feature by ticking Use this bucket to host a website.

At this point, you are asked to select the index document (in our case index.html) and the error document, since all routing managed by Vue router can directly use index.html or if you want to draw up a personalized error page change it with the necessary documentation.

Browsing now the URL <bucket-name>.s3-website-<AWS-region>.amazonaws.comwe will be able to see our application fully functional. It can, however, be noted that if we navigate a specific path without first going to the root of the site, the error page (if customized) or the application with the correct page but with an HTTP error code (403) will respond. This is because, inside the bucket, there is no folder required by the path.

To overcome this problem, we return to the Static website-hosting configuration, this time by adding Edit Redirection Rules to this text area

```
<RoutingRules>
<RoutingRule>
<Condition>
<HttpErrorCodeReturnedEquals>403</HttpErrorCodeReturnedEquals>
</Condition>
<Redirect>
<HostName>my-bucket-name.s3-website-eu-west-1.amazonaws.com</HostNam
<ReplaceKeyPrefixWith>#!/</ReplaceKeyPrefixWith>
</Redirect>
</RoutingRule>
</RoutingRules>
```

In this way, the path will be rewritten using the hash tag as a prefix and will be processed by the Vue router. We will now see the application working properly.

Static site optimization

The price of the S3 service is based on how much space we use and how many access requests we make to our files, with regard to the first parameter; there is no problem, a static web application is very light, about the second parameter can be a problem.

To optimize this cost and improve the speed of the site, it is better to use CloudFront to serve the content through the Edge locations or servers scattered around the world where the content will be replicated, and this allows users to download content from the server closest to them. Regarding the cost, the CloudFront price is based on the traffic that is served and is lower and better optimized than paying for the requests, as the website is very light you will see the difference in the billing.

Let's go than to create a CloudFront web distribution from the AWS console, among the thousand settings I dwell on the first: Origin Domain Name. Here you can select our bucket from the drop-down menu, and you need to pay attention to this aspect, connecting it in this way the S3 routing system will not work; so if you browse a path like /my-pageCloudFront, you will not be able to go and get the file /my-page/index.htmlas did S3.

In our case, it is not a problem because we have only one index.html inside the root of the site, so we can very well use this method and go to set Default Root Object as index.html (this applies only to the path /). And for the routing problem? The simplest solution is to modify the configuration in the Error Pages tab of our CloudFront distribution (it will be visible after creation) for the errors of 403 and 404 index.html. It is not a clean solution, in this case, personally, I prefer to use it as a solution and to set it as the origin HTTP directly to the endpoint of the static web site served by S3 <bucket name>.s3-website-<region>.amazonaws.com).

Pre-launch preparations

At this point in the configuration, I am satisfied with the result, the application works well, the application loading time remains below the second, and data access in DynamoDB is safe and very fast (60 / 70ms) and most important of all : up to this point, I spent 0 $

Being few in the accesses, I have always remained in the free tier of AWS that allows you, for one year to use the services free with very high thresholds; the application could run in beta version with few users with the cost always at 0. At the end of this year, the free thresholds are lowered, but in any case, during the test and staging phase, it is very difficult to reach 2 $ of billing.

What is missing before being able to open the service to the world?

Resource consumption

Serverless architecture gives a great advantage: this is the automatic scaling of resources. This means that if your service works with ten users, it will also work with 1,000, and with 1,000,000 users without problems, all you need is a nice platform configured for your credit card. CloudFront has no problems if the user load increases, as Cognito, being a managed service, we don't worry about it. You can configure DynamoDB instead both with fixed Throughput

Capacity and in autoscaling mode, where alone this value will increase and decrease.

The first concern that came to my mind was that, so I have no control over this scaling.

Serverless resource consumption

The first things that we can do to control scaling and resource consumption are to set a fixed DynamoDB Throughput Capacity, so that if traffic increases more than expected, requests are throttled or ignored. The AWS SDK will automatically retry the request by causing the frontend to slow down, perhaps more acceptable than having to pay heavy AWS invoices without having the necessary funds to cover them.

Metrics, metrics, and metrics

The most important thing is to monitor CloudWatch metrics for critical services such as Lambda, DynamoDB, API Gateway, CloudFront, and add alarms to be alerted via email if something is not working properly.

It is possible to create customized CloudWatch metrics based on application logs, saved in CloudWatch Logs; this is very convenient to have a better view of specific application functions. All Lambda function logs are automatically saved in CloudWatch Logs streams. A very nice feature of CloudWatch is to be able to create custom dashboards to insert graphics, change colors, add notes, and much more. Beware that each dashboard created will cost $ 3 a month, so be careful.

Profiling and analysis

If the application works a lot on the Lambda functions to respond to the APIs, process messages in the SQS queues react to DynamoDB events; it is good to keep this part monitored as much as possible. We must remember the main rule because it has so many functions and it's quick. It is better to perform many functions lasting a few milliseconds than a few minutes, and this would make the AWS bill rise very quickly.

I did an experiment by activating X-Ray (an analysis and debugging service) to my lambda functions. Using the Serverless framework was very simple; I installed the serverless-plugin-tracing plugin with npm

Npm install—save-dev serverless-plugin-tracing and then added to the project plugins: - serverless-plugin-tracing

Using the AWS SDK within the Lambda, the latter must be instrumentalized by modifying the inclusion of the module in const XRay = require ('aws-xray-sdk'); const AWS = XRay.captureAWS(require('aws-sdk')); without making any other changes to the code, in an instant, I found all the analysis of the application in a graphic and well-ordered manner within the AWS console.

This is an example of the result: aws x-ray

Billing alerts

Don't start using any AWS service before setting up billing alerts, and I find it a vital feature to be alerted if costs starts to rise.

I spent at least a couple of weeks not working continuously. Obviously, there were many changes of course and experiments. I, therefore, hope to have put you on the right track in case you want to try this experience for your project, in order to get the hang of it, whether or not you have all the architectural knowledge.

CHAPTER 6

Create A Vps Environment With Lightsail Without System Knowledge

For those who know or are aware of Amazon AWS services, the first thing that comes to mind is the difficulty and the number of different services to be set up and managed. Thinking of serving an increasingly independent audience, that also requires speed in getting their applications up and running, Amazon created Lightsail,

Amazon lightsail

To start using this service, we need to go to the AWS management console and select the Lightsail service you find in the group called Compute. You will be presented with a screen a little bit different from the standards of the other services, and this is precisely because the service has been designed to be easy and intuitive.

As you can see in the Help section, to start our first private server we must select an image, choose a plan (machine power and cost), give a name to our configuration, and press the "CREATE" button. Even if it's all very simple, let's see in more detail the features of each step:

Image: in a cloud-computing environment, this term indicates a binary image containing an operating system and the pre-installed software that will be used during the configuration and startup of a server. We find different types of images, those with only the operating system and the one with OS + Application. At the moment, there are products like WordPress, Magento, Joomla, Node.js, Drupal, etc.

Plan: at the moment, the service offers plans from \$ 5 to \$ 80 based on the characteristics of the server you want to buy. The Lightsail service has just come out, and most likely, other types of servers will be added in the near future.

Instance name

Once we have selected the information indicated, we must assign a name to our configuration, we must specify a unique name that will no longer be possible to change, to do so we should recreate a new configuration.

Instance creation

To test the Lightsail service and test the overall performance of the solution, let us choose an image with WordPress and the \$ 10 per month plan with a 1GB RAM server, 30 GB SSD and 2TB data transfer to compare it with the 5 $. After indicating all my options, click on the "create" button.

This is divided into two sections, which are the resources and snapshots. In the first, we find our instances (server), and as we will see later, the DNS domains that we want to manage directly from the service. In the second section, there are snapshots that are snapshots of our servers, which we can use as backup and restore and / or as initial images to start other private servers.

On each server in the list, we can see the associated name, the technical characteristics, the geographical region (Virginia), the availability zone (Zone A), the status of the service (running), and the IP address associated with the running instance. If we select the menu indicated with the three vertical dots, it is possible to restart, stop, and/or delete the server or enter the resource configuration or connect to the server via SSH.

SSH connection

The first operation that I recommend is to immediately run an SSH connection to the new server to check its operation and in our case take the password with which we could log in to the WordPress admin panel. To make the connection, choose the "connect" option from the instance menu, you do not need any client; the operation is via the browser.

Once inside the server, we check with the command "ps –ax" if all the processes that interest us are active, such as apache, mysql, and php, if all went well, then run this command to get the WordPress password: "cat bitnami_application_password"

NB: In this example, we executed a standard SSH connection, which is also the simplest to implement. However, know that we can also use our favorite client as putty or the native Linux system, to do this, when creating the server we must select an option indicated as Change SSH Key Pair with which we can create a new key or upload an existing one.

LOG IN TO WORDPRESS

Now that everything is ready, we just have to run the first login on our WordPress and check the basic configuration features, such as installed plugins, language, theme, and all the features to customize. As we have seen, in each instance, the public IP address is indicated, so we use this address with / wp-admin, and we try to execute our first login; we must use it as "user" and password the one taken in the previous chapter.

These are the plugins that we would find and are all installed after the first login; obviously, you are free to change things with maximum freedom, I suggest you keep WP-Mail-SMTP, which is already configured to send emails in a cloud-computing environment. Now you just need to install your favorite theme and do all the tests you want.

Since the software is installed via bitnami, I suggest you also read the documentation page that you find on your server by retrieving the indicated URL.

DNS MANAGEMENT

The operations we have performed so far are fine for general tests, but if we need to create a production environment, we probably need a domain name to associate with our instance. For by this we can act in different ways; for example, if we manage the domain from another supplier, it is sufficient to indicate in the DNS configuration of the provider for the association name domain and IP address that we find indicated in the resources screen. If we want to manage a DNS directly from Amazon Lightsail, we need to create a DNS zone.

To do this, just select the DNS Zone item from the "create other resources" menu, indicate the domain name you want to manage, and confirm the selection. At this point, you should find the new DNS resource on the general resource page.

Once you create the DNS zones, you can configure them with customized entries and associated domains and sub domains with any resources you want. Remember that if the current DNS is from an external provider, you must indicate the new name servers, in order to be sure that the valid entries will be those indicated in the Amazon Lightsail service.

Snapshots

Once we have the snapshot, we can use it to start a new instance or delete it, maybe because a new copy has overtaken it. Snapshots are also very useful for testing with new updates; for example, if we have our WordPress with all our plugins installed, our custom theme, etc., what should we do to try everything with a new version of WP? In the VPS environment, it is very simple, just create an instance starting from the snapshot, and you will get a server identical to the one of production, make the updates of the case and check the functioning, all without disturbing the production server in the least.

Static IP Addresses

As we saw in the previous chapters, when we start an instance, the system assigns a public IP address that we can use in a DNS entry to associate a domain name. The problem is that every time we stop the server, the Amazon Lightsail service assigns a new IP address to the machine. So we are obliged to update the DNS whenever this happens. To overcome this problem, it is sufficient to request a static IP address to be associated with the instance permanently.

To do this, just select the “create other resources " menu and choose the "Static IP" option, you will be asked for the name of the instance you want to associate with this new IP address and the service will perform the configuration in the way of all automatic, you won't have to worry about this problem anymore.

The Metrics

Many times, having a history of how our server is used can help us understand if the characteristics of the server chosen are right for our site or not. In the Amazon Lightsail service, it is possible to enter each instance and see graphs with which to analyze CPU consumption and data traffic entering and leaving the server.

In addition to the usage metrics, it is possible to check for any errors related to our system or instance. This is very useful in the sense that they would notify you in advance of a possible general failure of the instance, in fact, if we see that there are recurring system errors it is better to restart the instance and let us assign another virtual resource.

CHAPTER 7

Create A Cloud Storage Environment Through The Amazon S3 Service

The Amazon S3 storage service in the cloud is a great resource. It offers storage space, fast storage, and distributed access. It offers an automatic backup that allows you to transfer data or test websites without running into problems.

We will explain how to use Amazon CloudFront to execute files via CDN to speed up the download and latency of your website.

Detached Media

Detached media can simplify life. Imagine this situation: you would need to move your website to another server. If you have this need, it means that your website has become too big for the space you have available. You probably have so many images.

Within WordPress, each type of content takes up very little space for posts, themes, and plugins. Even for a very large blog, it takes a database of about 2-3 MB, which may be sufficient.

Probably your themes and plugins take up 10-30 MB, but you do not have to move many of these; you just simply need to download them again. Every time you upload an image to WordPress, at least three other versions are created (unless its size is very small). This means that for every image you upload, you will actually have four other images on your server. So for only 100 images, you'll have 400 images. Naturally, in this way, it is easy to exceed 400-600 MB.

Thanks to powerful development tools, you could transfer everything in WordPress in a few minutes, but then spend hours on media content. Furthermore, other inconveniences, such as upload/download timeout problems, would be added.

Instead, if you use a cloud-based storage service, it will provide all the media files from the cloud. There will be no need to think about the upload folder. In this way, the migration of a very large site could take only a few minutes. Another benefit you can get from this tool is the possibility to carry out tests. If the developers use a local environment to test, the images will work well as they will be taken directly from the Amazon servers, unlike WordPress, which must search them on a local hard drive.

Scalability

AWS has a huge capacity. It is not possible to create a site that Amazon's servers cannot support. Just think of Netflix, and it is just one customer who turned to Amazon. The scale possibility it offers cannot be underestimated.

Price

Another advantage of choosing AWS is the very low prices it offers. Moreover, taking advantage of the cloud service, you can simplify the economic management, which can be complex.

Security and control

Amazon's security is also extended, thanks to the addition of innovative data protection tools. Furthermore, the provider offers integrative solutions with S3 storage, such as, just to give an example, that of Check Point Software Technologies.

To start, you will need:

- AWS account and then later access S3 service;
- Security credentials generated;
- Amazon Web Services plug-in;
- Amazon S3 and Cloudfront plug-ins.

Amazon S3 account

With the S3 account, you will have access to the AWS management console, where you will find a list of all available Amazon services. Click on S3 and access the S3 management area. The interface is very similar to a file system. The buckets are the top-level directory, which can hold them within any number of files and directories. The name of the bucket you choose will have to be unique in S3, as in all AWS services, so do not use very generic names.

Security credentials

At the top of the navigation bar, select the account name and then on the menu item security credential. You will have access to Identity Access Management or IAM, where you will create a new user through the Create New Users function. You will be responsible for the interaction between Amazon and your website. Choose Users in the left sidebar and then click on the blue "Create New Users" button. It is also possible to create multiple users simultaneously.

Let's create a single user: amazontestuser.

Make sure you check the "Generate an access key" for each userbox before clicking the blue "Create" button. On the next screen, you will see the login credentials. It is important to take note of these credentials, as AWS will not show them to you in the future. In case you lose them, you will need to create a new user.

Configure Amazon S3

Make sure you install and activate the two plugins: Amazon Web Services and Amazon S3 and Cloudfront. Once done, you will see a menu item on the WordPress admin. Select it, and, in the tab, enter your security credentials. To test plug-ins quickly, you need to copy the ID of the Access key ID and the Secret Access Key we created earlier. So, it is necessary to move the keys to wp-config.php file for security. We will see later why it is sufficient to mark the values in the file. Select S3 and CloudFront items in the AWS menu. You can select a bucket from your account using the drop-down menu. Place all uploads in this bucket. We recommend checking the "Set item" for future HTTP expiration header, for upload file. In the second part of the box, check the entries: Copy to S3 as you upload and Point the URLs.

To sum up

We created a bucket on an S3 server to store your files and made sure that the URLs also pointed to this bucket. If you try to upload a file, you should see the URL pointing to Amazon instead of your domain. Unfortunately, they won't send you the pre-existing images automatically to S3 servers. On this subject, plugin developers are working on a pro version. A further step can help you further improve your users' experience by ensuring a faster service. Amazon CloudFront is a CDN (Content Delivery Network), which offers integration with other AWS products to facilitate developers and companies to distribute content to users with low latency. It allows a high data transfer speed and no minimum commitment to using. The CDN is a very useful tool because it allows you to serve images from a location that is geographically closer to the user. For example, if you have a server in the United States, a European reader will have a higher loading time than a US one. The CDNs addressed this very problem by reflecting the content on different locations in order to offer files from a location closer to the user.

Configuring CloudFront is quite simple

Go back to the Management Console in your Amazon S3 account, click on CloudFront. After activating this service, the following screen will appear. Click the "Create Distribution button," then choose to Get Started in the Web section. On the page, you will find settings; select the bucket created in Origin Domain Name. Scroll down and click on Create Distribution. The distribution will take 20-30 minutes to activate. Wait until the status is set to Enabled. Back in Amazon S3 with the Cloudfront plugin, and in the setting, in the CloudFront settings fill in the Domain name field. Amazon S3 is a great solution for storing media files. It is possible to move sites every time you need to scale applications and be simply without the fear of damage. Furthermore, the use of CloudFront reduces the download time, which could compromise the participation of its users.

CHAPTER 8

Create A Virtual Desktop Environment In The Cloud With Amazon Workspaces

Amazon WorkSpaces adopts a consumption approach, with a fixed monthly price for each desktop based on the features and licenses required. Those who choose to adopt a platform like this must not worry about licenses, at least as far as the fundamental applications and the operating system are concerned or performance, the platform is supplied turnkey and can also interface directly to all Amazon Web Services, to satisfy even the highest demands in terms of IT infrastructure.

WorkSpaces are available in three macro families of packages: Value, Standard, or Performance, all with the respective differences in terms of hardware and software resources. By default, all WorkSpaces bundles are equipped with a Windows 7 operating system or rather Windows 7 Experience based on Windows Server 2008 R2 with Internet Explorer 11 and WinZip, while access to Plus solutions allows you to start the virtual instance enriched with additional software Office Professional, Trend Micro, and a utility package. Once the WorkSpaces has started, it is possible to install the necessary software with the relevant licenses in the user's possession; alternatively (and regardless of the package chosen), a customized image can be created with respect to the standard ones.

Once you select the type of environment and deploy from the AWS web interface, users receive an email with instructions for accessing their virtual desktop. To be able to start using WorkSpaces, simply download the appropriate client and log in with the credentials, provided the client is available for PC, Mac, Chromebook, iPad, Kindle, and Android tablet, thus allowing full use and portability. Furthermore, the cloud-based nature of WorkSpace permits the user to switch from one device to another in a completely transparent manner and without losing access to its resources installed software, data, and so on. WorkSpaces integrates perfectly with an existing Active Directory platform if it is not already present in the company, an ad hoc domain is created to which all desktops are connected.

A very important aspect is that of security, by using the PC-over-IP protocol (PCoIP), the corporate data, or in general, the data of who administers the infrastructure are not in any way stored on the device in use by the end-user. In this way, the user experience is the most similar to that of a physical desktop. The protocol also takes care of optimizing bandwidth usage, without the data coming out of the AWS cloud and consequently from the environment of work.

The cost of the different packages also varies according to the geographical area to which they belong. Amazon also allows the use of proprietary licenses Windows and Office subject for verification of some minimum requirements, thus saving a few dollars, compared to normal prices. For example, a Value configuration with one vCPU, 2 Gbytes of Ram, 10 Gbytes of storage, costs $27 a month, the Standard configuration with 2vCPU, 4 Gbytes of Ram, and 50 Gbytes of storage comes to $ 37. Switching to the Plus version with Office Professional and the Trend Micro Worry-Free Business antivirus costs $ 15 more per month. The prices are unfortunately not divisible: even if you use the desktop for a couple of days, you will have to pay the whole month.

Sensations of use as an end-user

With the package $ 42 a month, once the WorkSpace Client is installed, it is sufficient to enter the credentials to find yourself working with an interface that is completely similar to that of the Windows Remote Desktop connection. It is also possible to work in full screen to eliminate the feeling of work on a remote desktop, even if you use two screens connected to the PC Workspaces fits on both screens at maximum resolution.

The overall user experience is good, although partially limited by the performance of the package 2GB of RAM and 1vCPU, which at times gives a feeling of non-optimal responsiveness. The navigation in the file system and in the different areas of the operating system is fluid; the launch of programs Word, Excel, Chrome, etc. requires an acceptable time, but of course, not at the level of those offered by a physical desktop with an SSD disk. These sensations have been confirmed by a performance test on storage, which seems rather modest values, while we were positively impressed by the speed of Internet connection, which exceeds abundantly 100 Mbps in download and 50 in upload traffic is billed separately based on AWS rates.

The local printers are all automatically hooked up and worked perfectly in our tests. To share files between desktops, you can then use WorkDocs: a managed object storage service with a very similar operation to Dropbox, for which the Android, iPad, and Kindle Fire versions are also available.

In our opinion, WorkSpaces has a winning approach to VDI. Certainly, it is suitable in many situations and offers many advantages compared to the setup of an on-premises infrastructure: ease of creation of work environments, scalability, security, and absence of maintenance are the main ones, even if updates of the operating system must still be the applied operator. Among the disadvantages, there is certainly the price, not particularly high, but definitely higher than that of the purchase of a laptop and the related licenses for even three-year use. If in the account, however, the costs of management, deployment, configuration, and administration of IT resources are put in place, the gap in terms of price would be convenient, at least for those who are satisfied with a traditional desktop that is not particularly attractive

CHAPTER 9

General Features And Benefits Offered By Amazon Web Services

Amazon started his online book sales business back in 1995 to end today, selling everything. To achieve this, Amazon did not only have to deal with marketing issues, but had to invest in the information system and the hardware base in order to manage a huge volume of traffic that was generated every day worldwide.

For this reason, in just a few years, there was an enviable networking infrastructure and a series of services called "Amazon Web Services " or AWS, designed and based on reliability, scalability, and speed. Amazon conceived this experience with in- house staff, as at the time there was no computer on sale capable of satisfying the traffic generated by the company in the Internet world.

If we want to understand the services available, we must assimilate two concepts well, one related to the Amazon Web Services also called AWS and the other on the networking structure. We will report description to clarify some concepts better, while immediately afterward; the services will be listed, divided by group, with the possible connection.

Definition of cloud computing

Many words have been spent trying to define the term cloud computing, and unfortunately, there is still a lot of confusion to try to understand what can be considered a cloud and what is not. Surely not all the services and technologies to which we are accustomed to accessing can be defined as cloud computing services.

The birth of Amazon Web Services

The real idea came in 2006, when Amazon understood that its infrastructure and its web services, which he used currently only for itself, could be shared with other companies that need a reliable infrastructure for their business. In a nutshell, he began selling cloud-computing technology many years ahead of any other IT services company.

Even the payment method is particular, in fact, you only pay for what you use, there are no fixed-rate contracts or fixed-rate tickets as we are used to seeing in hosting plans, even here as we would have seen, the advantages are many and can save significant amounts of money as compared to a proprietary structure.

Global networking structure

Amazon provided a number of data centers around the world; the terms geographic area and area of availability were used. The first identifies the physical area where the data centers of the resources we want to buy are located, while the second identifies the redundant centers that are present in the same geographical area.

For example, in the European geographical area of Ireland, we have three different availability zones, while in the USA, Virginia area, we have the possibility to choose four availability zones. For many services (like Amazon S3), it would be enough to select a geographical area, and the resources will be automatically replicated for the various availability zones we choose.

AWS edge locations

The choice of the geographical area on AWS is very important, as it influences the latency and, therefore, the response times, normally it is good to choose the nearest geographical area, the costs for the same service are different between Brazil, USA, Europe, etc., etc. Some services initially are not available for all geographical areas.

As for the distribution of content worldwide, such as static resources or some multimedia files such as streaming videos, Edge Locations are also used, which are infrastructures that are used for specific delivery functions, in such a way to approach requests and improve response times if you want to see the map go to Amazon Global Infrastructure.

Amazon Web Services

The services made available today are quite a few, also because Amazon's AWS section releases some news or new services every month. In any case, to facilitate selection, the AWS is divided into six different groups:

1. Compute: in this group, we find all the services for computing resources, therefore the management of virtual servers in EC2 cloud, the Lambda service for the execution of code following events on other AWS services or Container Service (ECS) facilitates the management of groups of instances with particular characteristics in common.

2. Storage: here, all the services related to storage and storage of large online data. In the list, we find the Amazon S3 storage service, storage designed for backups called Amazon Glacier, a direct connection solution without internet between company and cloud with Storage Gateway.

3. Database: through these services, we can manage databases without having to install specific software on our virtual servers and take advantage of the automatic scalability of Amazon. We can choose a NoSQL database like DynamoDB, a report database like MySQL and Microsoft SQL Server in RDS, RAM caching system in ElastiCache, and a high-speed Redshift data warehouse system.

4. Networking & CDN: in this group, we find the services concerning network resources. Therefore, the management of a DNS with Route 53, private resources with non-public servers and customizable VPC network, boundaries with Virtual Private Cloud, dedicated connections between company and Amazon AWS with VPN connection through Direct Connect, the distribution of static and multimedia content on different geographical regions with CloudFront.

5. Migration: in this section, there are Amazon services that provide for the migration of different resources; for example, we can migrate heterogeneous databases with the Amazon DMS service or move large amounts of corporate data with a hardware device called Snowball to be sent directly to the headquarters of Amazon.

6. Developer Tools: all services for supporting general programming and sharing source flows. Save the sources in a Private GIT with CodeCommit, manage the continuous release with CodePipeline, and automate the deployment with CodeDeploy.

Management Tools: these are all the services for the management aspects concerning the general management of the system. Check the performance indicators and activate automatic actions with CloudWatch, check the complete history on the current and historical configuration of your changes with Config, monitor API calls with CloudTrail, and get advice on resources from Trusted Advisor.

Security & Identify: these are services for general management and access control through security policies. Safely control and manage all access permissions with IAM, synchronize active directory with Directory Service, etc.

Analytics: here, we find the services that perform analyzes based on large data structures. The first service released is Elastic MapReduce, based on a framework called Hadoops, ideal for data warehousing. Other services that we find in this section are Data Pipeline and the latest Kinesis.

Artificial intelligence: in this group, we find several useful services for developers to integrate AI algorithms in their applications. For example, you can use the Amazon Rekognition service with which you can recognize objects or scenes in an image or the Amazon Polly service for the translation of a text in Audio format.

Internet of Things: AWS has created specific IoT services such as AWS Greengrass and AWS IoT. They will help you collect and send data to the cloud, facilitating the loading and analysis of this information and allowing you to manage your devices so that you can focus on developing applications that meet your needs.

Game Development: This group is dedicated to services for the development of professional video games, in which both the development tools and the necessary hardware resources are made available. For example, we find the Amazon GameLift service, the Amazon Lumberyard service, a multi-platform 3D game engine.

Mobile Services: in this section, there are services that can be used by mobile applications to perform specific tasks. Like identity management for logins and synchronizations with Cognito and mobile statistics with Mobile Analytics.

Application Services: here, we find all those services that we can use by directly calling specific applications that runs in the cloud without having to buy EC2 instances or online storage. For example, we have a particular search engine called CloudSearch, used for video conversions with Elastic Transcoder, job planning with SWF, and application development in a low-latency environment for gaming with AppStore.

Messaging: In the messaging group, we find all the Amazon services with which it is possible to manage message communications, for example, complete management of notifications between different supports with Amazon SNS, a mail delivery service with Amazon SES, and the distribution management of the workload through message queues with Amazon SQS.

Business Productivity: in this group, we find all the services for business applications, such as the service for the management of corporate email with

WorkMail and the management for documents with WorkDocs. Some of these services can be integrated into your company with clients released by Amazon.

Desktop & App Streaming: in this group, there are all the services that belong to desktop environments such as the Virtual Desktop service called WorkSpaces and the streaming application development service known as AppStream 2.0.

Compute

Compute & networking

EC2

A web service that provides data processing capabilities in the cloud provides through virtualization the possibility to choose different operating systems, services, and databases already ready. The service can be managed via a web console or via the API to be used in a programming environment. Amazon EC2 also provides a number of sub-services for the advanced management of our instance, such as traffic balancing, Auto Scaling, and more.

ECS Container Service

Amazon EC2 Container Service (ECS) is a high-performance, highly scalable container management service that supports Docker containers and allows you to run applications on a managed Amazon EC2 instance cluster easily.

Lightsail

With this new service, you can easily manage a VPS "Virtual Private Server" and start a web application with predefined images, such as WordPress, Joomla, Magento, Drupal, and more, in just a few minutes. To use this service, it is not necessary to have special system knowledge, and it is possible to start a server in production with a few simple steps.

Elastic Beanstalk

The Amazon EC2 service provides only computational power, which, once configured from a systemic point of view and with the addition of specific software, can run any application. For many, this results in inconvenience, because you have to take on all the problems related to the configuration of the instance before worrying about the application. This is precisely why Amazon has developed Elastic Beanstalk, which allows you to upload the application directly to AWS without worrying about other aspects.

Lambda

This service allows you to define functions that can call a particular code; you must execute it when an event occurs on AWS services. For example, if you edit a file on S3 if an element is inserted on DynamoDB or a message that comes to Amazon Kinesis. The peculiarity of this service is that we do not have to worry about scalability, for example, we do not care if there is a change in Amazon S3 per second or 100,000, the functions will continue to work and execute the code that will be assigned to it.

Batch

AWS Batch allows you to run easily and effectively hundreds of thousands of batch processing jobs on AWS. Dynamically providing the optimal amount and type of computing resources (CPU or memory) based on the volume and resource requirements specific to the batch jobs sent. With AWS Batch, there is no need to install and manage calculation software or server clusters to perform the work, and this allows you to focus on analyzing the results and solving problems.

Storage

S3

With this "storage" service, it is possible to store and recover large amounts of data, at any time and from anywhere on the web. It provides users with the ability to access the same highly scalable, reliable, and fast data storage infrastructure that Amazon uses to keep its network of websites up and running. This service can also be used as a secure form of backup, both for other AWS services like EC2, but also as a backup for corporate servers.

Elastic File System

It provides us with the scalable file storage for use with Amazon EC2 instances. Amazon EFS is easy to use and offers an interface that allows you to create and configure file systems quickly and easily. The service is designed to offer availability and durability, providing performance that meets a wide range of workloads, including Big Data applications.

Glacier

Unlike the Amazon S3 service, it represents a low-cost solution suitable for storing what concerns the backup functions. Surely, it is a great service for corporate network environments, but it can also be used for personal use instead of other services such as Dropbox, the important thing is to understand the differences well and check the cost table. This service has been designed to store information that normally should you should not download, except for recovery problems. If used in this way, the prices are very advantageous, and the cost is much lower as compared to S3, which is optimized for the publication of the contents and not only for their storage.

Storage Gateway

This service allows you to install in your local network software that takes care of the physical copy of the disks connected to the local servers in the storage environment on S3. If a disk should fail, we can quickly restore it from the Amazon S3 service and reboot the system to normal operation. If instead, we have a fault, we can start instances on EC2 and restore EBS snapshots, at least until normal recovery.

Database

Cloud & Database

RDS

A web service that offers complete management of a relational database such as MySQL, Oracle, Microsoft SQL, etc. and with which it is possible to integrate other AWS services, in addition to simplifying backup, resizing, and patching activities. With this service, we don't have to install and configure a database software on our EC2 instances, and we don't have to worry about data alignment, let alone scalability. All these aspects will be handled automatically by the Amazon RDS service.

DynamoDB

This service allows the complete management of a NoSQL database in a cloud-computing environment. This is an exceptional combination for scalability and the elimination of some limits in relational databases. This service was born after 15 years of experience with SimpleDB and Dynamo used on the Amazon.com website, which in any case, had limits on the size of the dataset. The DynamoDB service will have no size limits and will automatically replicate data on three data centers. The service also frees us from backup and recovery problems.

ElastiCache

With this service, we can easily manage a complex functionality such as a RAM caching cluster. This service is fully compatible with Memcached. In fact, on a Memcached cluster, it is necessary to deal with quite complex systemic steps, in addition to the fact that a lot of control maintenance and verification, in general, is required. With the Amazon ElastiCache service, all this management becomes much simpler and incredibly scalable. Cache servers with over 200G of available RAM can be generated with a few clicks.

Redshift

With this service, we can create a data warehouse system in just few minutes, and perform all the SQL database queries we need. With this solution, it is possible to reduce the initial costs of a data warehouse system and avoid the complexities associated with this type of solution. In fact, using the Redshift service, we can only think of storing our data and not worry about the complexity related to the hardware structure and the problems of maintaining very expensive infrastructure.

Networking & Content Delivery

Cloud & Networking

VPC

This is a secure connection between a company's infrastructure and the AWS cloud. Amazon VPC allows companies to connect their networks to Amazon Web Services resources through the VPN (a virtual private network) so that they can expand the functions through cloud technology. For example, we could delegate some very heavy processing functions to the servers started in the cloud, which, however, will be reachable only by our internal network and accessible only by company accounts.

CloudFront

CloudFront is a web service for "content delivery," which is the distribution of static content or streaming at high speed and with low latency. The configuration is very simple since the service is connected to Amazon S3, in fact, it is enough to associate the resource of a buckets to CloudFront, and automatically the resource will be replicated in the different "edge points" scattered around the world, which will be used to meet the demands that they will be closer.

Direct Connect

We know very well that one of the weak points for the cloud in the company, especially in Italy, is the connection and internet bandwidth. In fact, Amazon's services are much appreciated when it comes to public resources, while they are seen as more problematic when a private network needs to be implemented with VPN connections in the cloud. For companies that need a secure connection, it is possible to create a direct line between the company and the nearest Amazon data center without passing through the internet.

Route 53

Route 53 is a fast and reliable DNS service that manages the corporate network or the resources present in Amazon Web Services like Amazon EC2 or S3. With this service, you can manage an unlimited number of domains and use Load Balancing features, using the Weighted Resource Record Sets technique. Obviously, you can also use this service for a private network or for the management of domains that you have in other registers. The advanced Health Check control options and the possibility to buy or transfer domains are also provided.

Migration

Data migration

Application Discovery Service

This service helps system managers to quickly plan for application migration by automatically identifying applications running in local data centers, as well as dependencies and performance profiles. This information is stored with encryption in the AWS Application Discovery Service database, which can be exported as a CSV or XML file for use on different cloud migration solutions.

DMS (migration)

Database Migration Service helps to migrate a database in a simple way. The source database will remain operational even during the migration to minimize the interruptions of the applications that use it. Database Migration Service allows you to migrate data to and from most of the most used commercial and open source databases. The service supports both homogeneous migrations, for example, from Oracle to Oracle, and heterogeneous migrations between different database platforms, for example, from Oracle to Aurora or from Microsoft SQL Server to MySQL.

Server Migration

AWS Server Migration Service (SMS) is an agent-less service that simplifies and speeds up the migration of thousands of local AWS workloads. This service allows you to automate, schedule, and monitor incremental replicas of active server volumes, making it much easier to coordinate large-scale server migrations.

Snowball

This particular service allows large amounts of data to be moved to the cloud using a hardware component made available by Amazon instead of internet bandwidth. Each appliance can hold 50 terabytes of data, and you can request several tools to perform a parallel backup. We can reduce several days of internet transfer to 48-hour operations and follow the entire ordering, shipping, and recovery process through management consoles.

Developer Tools

Cloud developer

CodeStar

CodeStar allows you to develop, build, and distribute applications in AWS. This service offers a unified user interface that simplifies the management of development activities. With AWS CodeStar, you can set up a continuous distribution tool-chain in just a few minutes, which speeds up code distribution. AWS CodeStar simplifies the collaboration of the development team and enhances security since it allows you to manage access with maximum simplicity and set up project owners, as well as who can modify it or just view it.

CodeCommit

CodeCommit is a fully managed source-code control service, which simplifies the corporate hosting of private GIT repositories in a secure and highly scalable way. CodeCommit eliminates the need to manage your source control system or to worry about resizing its infrastructure. CodeCommit provides storage capabilities, such as source code and binary code, and integrates seamlessly with existing GIT tools.

CodeBuild

CodeBuild is a self-managed service for compiling source code, running tests, and producing software packages ready for deployment. With this service, it is not necessary to configure and manage servers for any power level required. With this service, the processes run in parallel, and the necessary scalability is managed directly by Amazon, producing an always-performing result.

CodeDeploy

This service automates the deployment of an application present on EC2 instances. AWS CodeDeploy simplifies and speeds up the release of new features, helps avoid downtime during distribution, and manages the complexity of updating applications. You can use this service to automate distributions, eliminating manual operations subject to errors, and scalability management in order to use the same software distribution technique to an instance or thousands.

CodePipeline

CodePipeline is a continuous distribution service used to update applications quickly and reliably. CodePipeline creates, tests, and distributes the code every time it is modified, based on custom models and processes configured by the user. This allows you to distribute quickly and reliable features and updates. It is possible to create a complete solution with maximum simplicity using the pre-installed plug-ins of third-party services such as GitHub.

X-Ray

The service helps developers analyze and debug production and distributed applications such as those created with microservice architecture. With X-Ray, you can identify the performance of your application and related services to identify and resolve the root cause of problems and performance errors.

Management Tools

Cloud & Developer

CloudWatch

One of the fundamental aspects to keep under control after developing an application or a web service is to monitor performance through monitoring, not only for what concerns the use of disks or the CPU, but also for many other parameters. Amazon CloudWatch is the monitoring and alarm solution from Amazon Web Services. The use of Simple Notification Service (SNS) allows the sending of alarms via various supports that can be activated when a pre-set threshold is reached, so be notified immediately.

CloudFormation

With Cloudformation, it is possible to create templates with a JSON structure, which allows the creation of predefined configurations, that you can use to start and configure AWS resources that serve an application. For example, we could prepare a template that configures the start of a new instance with an operating system, decide the software to install and start additional services. To date, there are several templates for configurations of all kinds, for example, templates for WordPress, Drupal, and Joomla.

CloudTrail

AWS CloudTrail is a service that records all API calls generated by any source, such as consoles or applications and writes log files. The callers, call time, source IP address, request parameters, and response items returned by the AWS service are recorded. The AWS API call history produced by CloudTrail allows a complete security analysis and tracking of AWS resource change.

Config

This service provides an inventory of our resources, lists configuration history, and notifications of any changes. With Config, it is possible to discover existing resources, export an inventory with all the configuration details, and always determine how and when a resource has been configured in any period.

OpsWorks

OpsWorks is an application management service created to facilitate those who uses DevOps development model, more info on Wikipedia. OpsWorks can automatically scale the application and keep the infrastructure healthy by replacing the instances that are blocked. OpsWorks, unlike Beanstalk, offers more flexibility and control, allowing you to customize the types of servers and services used.

Service Catalog

Service Catalog allows organizations to create and manage catalogs of IT services approved for use in AWS. Such IT services can include everything from images of virtual machines, servers, software, and databases to entire architectures for multi-level applications. The service allows you to check the available IT services and their versions, the configuration of available services, and access via permissions by individuals, groups, departments, or cost centers.

Trusted Advisor

With this service, it's like having a personal cloud expert, and it helps you to improve resources following best practices. Inspect the AWS environment and find opportunities to save, improve system performance and reliability, or help fill security gaps. Since 2013, customers who use it have received over 1.7 million recommendations and achieved more than $ 300 million in cost reductions.

Managed Services

Automate frequent tasks such as change requests, monitoring, patch management, security, and backup, as well as providing comprehensive lifecycle services to manage infrastructure provisioning, execution, and support. AWS Managed Services improves agility, reduces costs, and relieves manual infrastructure management tasks that typically distract valuable resources from the core business.

Security & Identify

Cloud & Security

IAM

Through this service, it is possible to control and securely manage access to AWS services and resources by its users. Using IAM, you can create and manage users and groups and use permissions to allow and/or deny access to resources. The IAM service also allows integration with existing users in your company network, and it also provides a series of APIs for customization and authorization management through procedural programs, it will be possible to manage users, roles, permissions, and credentials.

Inspector

Amazon Inspector is an automated security service that helps improve the security of a system and the compliance of applications deployed in AWS. Amazon Inspector examines applications for vulnerabilities or divergences from best practices. After performing an exam, Amazon Inspector provides a detailed list with the evaluation results, sorted by severity level.

Certificate Manager

Certificate Manager is a service that simplifies the purchase and management of SSL certificates for use with AWS services. You can use the SSL / TLS certificates to secure network communications and establish the identity of Web sites on the Internet. You can quickly request a certificate, distribute it on AWS such as Elastic Load Balancing load balancers or Amazon CloudFront distributions, and allow AWS Certificate Manager to manage certificate renewals.

Directory Service

This service allows you to link resources on AWS between an on-premise environment of Microsoft Active Directory and a stand-alone environment in the cloud. Connecting to a local directory is simple, and once the connection is established, all users can access resources and applications using existing credentials. It is also possible to launch directories based and managed on

Samba in minutes, making it easier to manage Windows workloads using the Amazon cloud.

WAF & Shield

WAF is a firewall that helps protect Web applications from exploits that can affect application availability, compromise security, or consume unauthorized resources. Through the WAF service, it is possible to select customized security rules that allow defining the permitted traffic. While the part concerning Shield, deals with problems related to DDoS.

Analytics

Cloud & Analytics

Athena

This service allows you to query objects in an S3 bucket with a SQL compatible language. This avoids the forcing of all those complex scripts to write many times in order to manage the objects in S3. Athena is a serverless service and does not need any infrastructure for executing queries that will be executed by a batch system in Amazon AWS.

Elastic MapReduce

MapReduce is a framework introduced by Google for distributed computing on large amounts of data in computer clusters. The Map () node takes the problem request, and the resolution algorithm divides it into many different sub-problems and distributes them to different nodes. The Reduce () node takes the answers of all the sub-problems and prepares the answer. In Amazon, you can experiment with this technique with all the nodes we need and test the speed of our resolution algorithm.

CloudSearch

This service allows users to search for content within applications or websites quickly and effectively. CloudSearch technology is the same used by Amazon.com for product-related searches, and the service tries to make developers who want to integrate research into their sites, released from the logic of public search engines. Using this service, developers can create their own search domain, store all the information in a database, and customize all search queries with the results list.

Elasticsearch Service

Elasticsearch is a managed service that simplifies the distribution, operation, and resizing of Elasticsearch in the AWS cloud. Elasticsearch is a well-known open-source search and analysis engine, ideal for analytical processes, real-time monitoring of applications, and analysis of clickstream data. Through the Management Console, you can set up and configure the Amazon Elasticsearch cluster in minutes.

Kinesis

This is a fully managed service for real-time processing of large-scale streaming data. Kinesis can continuously capture and store terabytes of data from hundreds of thousands of sources, such as websites, financial transactions, social media, etc., etc. With Kinesis Client Library (KCL), it is possible to build applications and use streaming data to feed real-time dashboards, generate alerts, and implement price and advertising dynamics.

Data Pipeline

This service allows you to process and move data between different AWS services and from on-premise data sources at specific intervals. With the Data Pipeline, you can access your data, transform them, process them, and then transfer the result to the various services: Amazon S3, RDS, DynamoDB, or MapReduce. With the Data Pipeline, you can define databased workflows so that current activities depend on completing previous tasks.

Quicksight

Quicksight is the Amazon Business Intelligence service, and you can import the data you want to analyze from different sources, such as Redshift, Amazon RDS, Amazon S3, third party sources, CSV files, and much more. Once you acquire the data, a very powerful engine called SPICE will process it, which will allow you in obtaining the results in graphic format with a few seconds of processing even on much data.

Artificial intelligence

Artificial intelligence

The former

Lex is a new Amazon AWS service for creating and writing a BOT for automatic conversation management using both text and voice. The design of this tool was to help all developers to integrate these complex algorithms easily and quickly into their applications, in both desktop and mobile environments.

Polly

With Amazon Polly, it is possible to translate a written text into a voice file that will use a spoken language, so it will not only be a translation into a voice but will be a true interpretation of the text that will make it a real spoken voice. In the console of this service, you will find several examples with which to start doing general tests.

Rekognition

Amazon Rekognition is an automatic image recognition service using different artificial intelligence algorithms. The use of the service is very simple, and the ease of its use would surprise you. Simply store an image on an S3 bucket calling an API and reading the result in JSON format.

Machine Learning

Amazon Machine Learning is a service that allows developers with any skill level to use the brand new Machine Learning technology with ease. This service offers visualization tools and guided procedures that help you complete the Machine Learning (ML) model creation process without having to learn complex ML technologies and algorithms.

Internet of Things

Internet of things

AWS IoT

The service called AWS IoT is a platform that allows connected devices to interact easily and securely with cloud applications and other devices. AWS IoT can support billions of devices and thousands of billions of messages and can process and route of those messages to AWS endpoints and other devices in a secure and reliable manner.

Greengrass

This software allows you to perform calculations, messaging, and data caching locally for the devices. With Greengrass, connected devices can perform AWS Lambda functions, keep device data synchronized, and communicate securely with other devices, even when not connected to the Internet.

AWS IoT button

It is a programmable button based on the Amazon Dash Button hardware. This single WI-FI device is simple to configure and designed to allow developers to start using AWS IoT, AWS Lambda, Amazon DynamoDB, Amazon SNS, and many other Amazon Web Services without having to write specific code.

Game Development

Videogames

GameLift

Amazon GameLift is a new service that allows you to distribute, manage, and recalibrate multi-player session-based video games by reducing the amount of time needed to create multi-player back-ends from thousands of hours to minutes. Available to developers using Lumberyard, GameLift is built on a cloud infrastructure that allows for rapidly expanding or reducing the capacity of game servers based on demand, without the need for additional programming costs.

Lumberyard

Multi-player games created with Lumberyard, a free multi-platform 3D game engine integrated with Amazon AWS and Twitch, are ready for use with the Amazon GameLift service, which reduces the technical risks that often push programmers to eliminate cloud-based multi-player features from their projects.

Mobile Services

Cloud & Mobile

Mobile HUB

The Mobile Hub service allows you to add new features easily to your applications for mobile devices, such as authentication, data storage, backend logic, push notifications, content distribution, and analysis. After creating the application with Mobile Hub, you can test it on real devices using control panels that allow you to monitor the use of the application.

Cognito

Amazon Cognito simplifies saving user data, such as app preferences or the current state of a game. You can do everything without writing backend code and without managing a complex infrastructure. You can save user data locally so that applications work even when they are offline.

Device Farm

The Device Farm service allows you to improve the quality of your iOS, Android, and Web apps, by testing them on real mobile devices in the AWS cloud. Unlike emulators, physical devices provide very detailed information about how users interact with the app because they allow other factors to be taken into accounts such as memory, CPU usage, and many other features.

Mobile Analytics

With this service, it is possible to collect, view, and understand the usage data of a large-scale application. Many analysis solutions related to mobile apps give statistics after several hours of the occurrence of events. This service is designed to provide a complete report only 60 minutes after receiving the data.

Pinpoint

With this service, you can easily manage campaigns in a mobile environment by defining the user target, the messages you want to send, and much more. Amazon Pinpoint can help you determine who to send push notifications to and decide when to send them, all with an integrated system that will allow you to check campaign results.

Application Services

Cloud & Services

Step Functions

With this service, it is possible to manage the execution of one's code and / or microservices using a visual workflow. You can add or remove steps without the need to rewrite the source code. The service will generate a log for each step status, so it will be easier to find a bug.

SWF

Through this service, it is possible to create a flow controller to coordinate the execution of various tasks according to a predefined logic in a cloud environment. This peculiarity allows the saving on the writing of code that should keep under control all the phases of a workflow that, however, it's managed by different machines and different processing environments. The Simple Workflow service takes on this complexity and automatically decides the tasks to be processed based on the individual answers of each single processing unit.

API Gateway

API Gateway is a fully managed service that simplifies the creation, publication, maintenance, monitoring, and protection of APIs on any scale to developers. With just a few clicks, the AWS Management Console can create an API that acts as a gateway through which applications can access data, business logic, or back-end service features.

Elastic Transcoder

Amazon Elastic Transcoder is a service that allows video conversion, and it is not a service suitable for the conversion of personal movies, which we can do with any software installed on the PC, here we are talking about developing an application capable of converting a video of input. This peculiarity would make it easy to view a video stored in the cloud between different devices such as Smartphone, tablets, and PCs.

Messaging

Messaging

SQS

Amazon SQS is one of the very first services released by Amazon, which allows the distribution of operations and, therefore, of workload through message queues present on one or more servers. For example, we could have a server that analyzes a web page and inserts in a queue the references to all the images on this page. The queue is analyzed by a series of other servers that can divide the workload and mark the end message as processed.

SNS

This service is a very important component of AWS services and allows notification of messages through different media. SMS support has been added, while Email, data queues, and HTTP / HTTPS messaging have been active for some time. It delivers messages to applications or users by eliminating polling in apps. It sends messages to individual devices or collectively to multiple destinations.

SES

This service allows the sending of emails via the infrastructure, without the need for dedicated servers or workstations. This is definitely a service system dedicated to companies that need to do marketing via e-mail or have to manage large mailing lists. Those who use the EC2 service can take advantage of up to 2000 free emails per day.

Business Productivity

Cloud & Enterprise

WorkDocs

This service is a document storage solution that also adds collaboration features between different users of the company. Once the documents have been stored in this service, you can consult them from different platforms. In fact, in addition to the classic web application, we can use all Android and iOS devices.

Workmail

Through WorkMail, it is possible to manage a complete e-mail environment with the management of a calendar and contacts. The Amazon WorkMail service is compatible with the standard Microsoft protocol and can be used with the well-known Outlook client. You can also integrate the service with standard e-mail applications on iOS, Android, and Microsoft Windows Phone devices.

Connect

It is a self-managed cloud-based call center service. The service is based on the same technology used by Amazon's customer service partners worldwide to communicate with millions of customers. The self-managed graphical interface in Amazon Connect also allows novice users to create contact flows, manage agents, and monitor performance parameters.

Chime

You can use Amazon Chime for online meetings, video conferences, calls, chats, and share content, both inside and outside the organization. Amazon Chime allows you to work productively from anywhere. You can encrypt all your communications, the chat history is never stored on your devices, and you can limit your meetings to see who participates.

Desktop & App Streaming

Desktop

Workspaces

This service is a valid alternative to structures based on VDI (Virtual Desktop); in fact, it provides a complete desktop environment in the cloud where it is possible to choose different types of configuration. Amazon WorkSpaces also supports the use of Microsoft's active directory service for user authentication.

AppStream 2.0

Amazon AppStream 2.0 is an application streaming service that provides users with instant access to their desktop applications from anywhere and on any device. The Amazon AppStream 2.0 service simplifies management, improves security, and reduces costs by moving a company's applications from their users' physical devices to the AWS Cloud.

CHAPTER 10

Independently Manage A Cloud Architecture Through Aws Services

Amazon AWS is a container of heterogeneous services, each of which, however, integrates with others to offer developers, companies, and each customer all the tools necessary to satisfy their computational needs. Given the incredible amount of services made available by Amazon and the innovations that this multinational company is able to propose every month, being able to treat them all in an adequately in-depth manner is not possible in a single intervention by a guide who nonetheless aims to deepen the practical aspects of the most used services. Thus, in the following, it was decided to offer all patrons an intelligent overview of the services, with a brief description for each of them.

The roundup wants to be intelligent, as it tries to give a logical structure in presenting the services, ascribing each service to its own area of competence, with the aim of making it clear that every Web Services exists within a much more complex structure complex and best organized.

Amazon AWS services

The architecture of Amazon Web Services is in itself very simple and starts from the bottom, indicating the entire global infrastructure of AWS to reach them through the different services, which is a high part of management and administration. It allows anyone, even those who are completely fasting from cloud computing, to enter the world of Amazon AWS on tiptoe, without confusion and with a minimum of confidence in their abilities.

Thus, we begin to understand how to move, what services to address for every type of need, and how these are classified and distinguished, even though they are interconnected.

The infrastructure

The AWS global infrastructure section is important to mention, as those who catalog services often forget it. In reality, the AWS infrastructure is itself a service, and it is no coincidence than to understand everything that comes next, a beginner must initially understand how the AWS network is structured. Going into more detail, we can divide Amazon AWS infrastructure into regions, availability zones, and edge locations. By learning to understand the differences, you immediately realize how Amazon AWS can help customers support applications that are tolerant of failure and adverse events, without interrupting the services offered.

Amazon AWS region services

In the map shown here, the Regions are indicated with squares in transparent blue. In practice, each Region is an independent set of AWS resources, geographically isolated from one another and scattered in some of the key territories of the world. Each Region is born with a specific intent to guarantee the right conditions of privacy and compliance. Right from the start, you will have to deal with them, as not all services are always available in the different regions in which AWS is divided. Currently, the Regions are 8, plus a Region GovCloud, but it is reserved for government agencies only. To choose a Region, you usually find the one that is closest to the end-users, i.e., those who will use the application implemented on AWS services. So, if you intend to develop an app for only Italian or European users, my advice is to rely on the Region located in Ireland. Furthermore, it may happen that the price of using a service varies according to the chosen Region.

Within each Region, the so-called Availability Zones exists. These regions are the independent areas that do not share any failure points with each other, and they all connect to each other through a low latency network. The zones are thought of as real backup systems, since, however unusual, faults can always occur. Customers, therefore, have the opportunity to develop their own app on different Zones in the selected Region and if failure occurs in a specific Zone, the application would remain online, thanks to the implementation and presence of the other zones. In the initial map, it displays the different Zones as blue squares belonging to the Regions.

Finally, although it should not be dealt with directly, it is also good to introduce the third structure of the network, namely "the Edge Locations." Think of supporting DNS services offered through Route 53 Web Services and CloudFront's CDN (Content Delivery Network), and the Edge Locations, making it possible to distribute content and apps to national users with reduced latency. In the BelPaese, the national Edge Location is located in Milan.

Above the infrastructure, there are networking services. These include three main services: Amazon Route 53, Amazon Virtual Private Cloud (VPC), and Amazon Direct Connect.

Networking services

Amazon Route 53. It is the DNS service offered by Amazon and translates the URL typed by users in the browser into the IP address associated with a resource. It is characterized by speed, reliability, and automatic scalability based on the volume of requests. The support of Edge Locations and the ability to perform domain name resolutions with low latency guarantees the speed. There is a strict link of reliability to the opportunity to implement fail-over rules based on the control of network services (Health Check). Recently, ELB support has also been introduced for DNS failovers. The DNS service is integrated with the other AWS services, and with the IAM (Identity and Access Management) service, which in the US East and GovCloud regions only allows fine control of DNS access. You can also use this service to manage a private network or a series of domains registered with other providers. The cost of Route 53 is calculated based on the number of domains used and based on the resolution queries that are made.

Amazon Virtual Private Cloud (VPC) is a way to expand the IT infrastructure inside your company, assigning a series of computational and application tasks to the cloud of AWS services, allowing them to run on Amazon's virtual servers. These servers will be made accessible only from the network and from company accounts. It leaves the customer with full control of the network, from the selection of IP address ranges to the configuration of routing tables and gateways, to the creation of subnets, to the opportunity to create security groups, to control the entry, and exit of servers cloud. The connection between internal company resources and those available in the cloud takes place via VPN (Virtual Private Network), based on Internet Protocol Security (IPSec). For the use of VPCs, there are normally no additional costs to that of the EC2 computing service.

Direct Connect. To connect the company to the cloud of AWS services, it is necessary to clash with the very low quality of the Italian connection lines, which are always poor in bandwidth, creating many problems in the implementation of a VPN between company resources and those offered by AWS. To get around this, customers can take advantage of a direct line between the company and the nearest Amazon data center, so they can extend their internal infrastructure without the hassles of Internet traffic.

Computing services

Amazon EC2 (Elastic Compute Cloud) is at the heart of Amazon Web Services, Amazon EC2 is the Web service designed to provide computing and data processing capabilities in a scalable cloud environment. In practice, the service is addressed to all developers or, in general, to all customers who cannot afford the necessary infrastructure to provide their own application on capital account and who, in the future, will not have the opportunity to manage sudden loads computational. Thus, instead of waiting for the implementation of new physical servers, with the resulting costs, the developers only need to interact with a simple interface (the AWS Management Console), which allows you to obtain and upload new cloud servers in just few minutes, allowing the user to increase or decrease the computational capacity distributed according to need.

Amazon AWS console

Not surprisingly, the service is called Elastic, as it allows immediate scalability and payment of the resources used, according to the most exquisite pay-per-use model. The elasticity, therefore, allows the commissioning of one of the hundreds of virtual servers simultaneously and within a few minutes, controlling everything from specific APIs or from a Web interface. Each server is then given complete control, as access takes place in root or Administrator mode, leaving the full user control of the cloud servers started. Flexibility is instead guaranteed by the opportunity to choose the most suitable hardware for your needs, thus allowing you to choose the land size of storage, RAM, and CPU, as well as the image of the operating system (Windows or Linux - with or without applications) more suited to the needs. The Amazon Machine Image (AMI) service allows you to save your configurations as images to replicate the cloud server from an environment that is ready for your business. The integration with other AWS services, such as Amazon Simple Storage Service (S3), Amazon Relational Database Service (Amazon RDS), Amazon SimpleDB, Amazon Simple Queue Service (Amazon SQS) allows you to provide a complete solution for the calculation, the query processing, and storage in a wide range of applications. Furthermore, it is possible to monitor certain metrics published on Cloud Watch.

Amazon Auto Scaling is the system that allows you to program automatically the scalability of the EC2 solution, varying the number of cloud servers based on the metrics collected by Cloud Watch, to maintain peak performance, and decrease usage costs during breaks. The customer has the possibility to define a series of alarms that trigger the preset self-scalability policies. The configuration of the Auto Scaling service takes place via API or command line, and whenever the default policies come into action, you would receive notifications through the Amazon Simple Notification Service (SNS). You can perform Auto Scaling at no additional cost.

Amazon ELB - Elastic Load Balancing. The design of this service is to distribute incoming traffic on different cloud servers belonging to different Availability Zones. This distribution takes place both based on the volume of requests to be managed and on the correct functioning of the individual cloud servers. Thus, if a cloud server is down or fails, it is excluded from balancing, at least until it is re-enabled. You can connect the Load Balancer to the Internet by assigning a public IP address, or it can be internal without public IP. ELB supports SSL and IPv4 but is also fully compatible with IPv6. The operating metric of ELB is always published on Cloud Watch, and its cost is based on the time in which each single ELB is active and on the size of the data exchanged through it.

Amazon AWS ELB

Storage services

Amazon Simple Storage Service (S3). It is the online storage service designed to have 99.999999999% durability. The data are organized in objects with a maximum size of 5 TB each, but without having any type of limit on the maximum number of objects that can be stored. The objects, in turn, are organized in Bucket. All stored data can be accessed at any time and from anywhere on the globe. The storage service is reliable, scalable, and fast to the point that Spotify itself has relied on this service for its (infinite, Ed) storage needs. Each object is protected with 256-bit AES encryption, and the accesses are controlled in a granular way through the possibility of setting a series of permissions. Each operation on objects or buckets is recorded in special logs and notifications can be received for the most important events. Of every object, the system stores all the versions and automatically eliminates the oldest objects. You can also design Amazon S3 to host static pages of a website to which you can redirect users to view a courtesy site if you can't reach the main portal for any reason.

Amazon Elastic Block Store – EBS is a special lesson that will be dedicated to this service in the near future. For now, it is sufficient to know that these are the volumes (raw or formatted) that can be associated with the different cloud servers of the EC2 service.

Amazon Glacier is a low-cost backup solution, which does not require initial investments and, unlike S3, its better suited to storing information for backup functions. This service is designed for data that is not accessed frequently, except in conditions of extreme necessity. It has a cost of $ 0.01 / GB / month and allows you to take advantage of the same durability as the S3 service without the need to do the planning of the necessary capacity, as the capacity increases on demand based on the amount of data. The cost is much lower than S3 because the design of the service is only for storing data and not for publishing content, as is the case for S3.

Finally, although it should not be dealt with directly, it is also good to introduce the third structure of the network, namely the Edge Locations. Think of supporting DNS services offered through Route 53 Web Services and CloudFront's CDN (Content Delivery Network), and the Edge Locations make it possible to distribute content and apps to national users with reduced latency. In the BelPaese, the national Edge Location is located in Milan.

Above the infrastructure, there are networking services. These include three main services: Amazon Route 53, Amazon Virtual Private Cloud (VPC), and Amazon Direct Connect.

CHAPTER 11

Create A Computing Infrastructure Using Scalable Virtual Servers

Cloud computing allows companies and organizations to access IT infrastructures in a new way, regardless of the concept of ownership and investment. With the Cloud, the paradigm of how applications are released is totally changed: we pass from a vertical to horizontal writing, where the power of the machine (whether physical or virtual) increases to the need, without the user being aware of it and allowing absolutely better performance.

This is why it is important to consider the Cloud infrastructure: this does not only represent a new technological architecture but a new way of thinking about IT, based on fruition rather than the possession of resources. This greater flexibility allows companies to free human and economic resources and capacities, with a view to promoting new innovative digital projects, as well as offering better support to business initiatives and the promotion of new operating models. Cloud computing can, therefore, bring great advantages in terms of savings and efficiency, and, on a higher value scale, offer the opportunity to innovate products and services, through scalable and measurable models that lend themselves to the development of new business.

The e-commerce company records a decisive increase in activity on some particular days, for example, black Friday or at certain times of the year, such as the sales or Christmas period. The increase in access to the site entails the need for an increase in computing power and memory, with the risk otherwise of losing opportunities. The ideal is, therefore, to have a system available that performs scaling, and this is achieved thanks to the Cloud. Thanks to the Cloud, in fact, if it is necessary to increase the computing power, it is possible to rely on the auto-scale!

This is important for all companies that sell online services, as the intention is that customers always find themselves in excellent condition when they make purchases, and the possibility of increasing the CPU and the memory available will certainly have a positive effect on the performance of the service offered.

The infrastructure agent and the downloaded package allow you to deploy multiple infrastructure monitoring extensions at a time. The download contains the infrastructure agent and the extensions that can be distributed to provide data on infrastructure components.

Amazon Storage Gateway is a service that directly connects your IT environment with a storage infrastructure in Amazon Web Services through a software appliance to be installed in your company. This allows the secure storage of your data in the AWS cloud system resulting in scalable and convenient storage. Amazon Storage Gateway offers two different types of storage, one based on volumes and the other based on tape.

Memorization Models

The service provides two storage models, one based on volumes and the other on tapes, the possible configurations are different, and in this article, we will try to analyze the most important ones:

Volume Gateway - provides storage volumes that can be mounted as simple iSCSI devices and configured without major problems in servers within your company. The volume configuration mode:

Volumes Gateway-cached

Volumes Gateway-stored

Gateway-virtual tape library (VTL) - provides a virtual tape infrastructure for backing up data in Amazon S3 or long-term archiving in Amazon Glacier that allows considerable cost reduction for this type of operation.

Cached volumes

In this case, the data is stored in the Amazon S3 service (simple storage service), and only a copy of the data with more frequent access is kept in the local storage. The operation is exactly like a cache system. Gateway cached volumes basically offer real savings on the total costs of primary storage and minimize the need to scale storage within your company, while maintaining low latency to access the most used data.

Storage gateway

At this moment in the cached gateway, the volumes can go from a minimum of 1GB to a maximum of 32TB and must be rounded to the Gigabyte. Each gateway that is configured as a cached volume, gateway can support up to 20 volumes for a maximum capacity of 150TB. When application server data is sent to volumes in AWS, the gateway initially stores this data on local disks called cache storage before uploading them to Amazon

S3. The cache storage acts as permanent storage for data that is waiting to be loaded into the Amazon S3 environment.

Stored volumes

When low latency is required for the entire data set, the gateway can be configured so that all data is stored locally, and an asynchronous backup is made in S3 via a series of snapshots. This type of configuration provides a reliable and inexpensive off-site backup, which can be restored locally. If you also need to replace your infrastructure in the event of disaster recovery, you can start EC2 instances.

Storage Gateway

Data written by the stored volume gateway is stored on local disks within the company, while asynchronously; a backup is performed in Amazon S3 in the form of an EBS snapshot. The size of the volumes goes from a minimum of 1GB to a maximum of 1TB. Each gateway configured as a stored volume gateway supports up to 12 volumes, for a maximum capacity of 12 TB. To prepare data on Amazon S3, the gateway stores data within the upload buffer. The gateway uploads the data in the upload buffer through an SSL connection into the active AWS Storage Gateway service in the AWS cloud. Then the service stores the encrypted data in Amazon S3.

Virtual tape library

With this function, it is possible to store all the backup files in Amazon Glacier and then take advantage of an economical backup system and long-term data storage. The system is compatible with most existing backup software in both Linux and Windows and provides a virtual tape system that scales without difficulty according to the needs of your company, completely eliminating the problem of managing, maintaining, and scaling a complex infrastructure of physical tape.

Storage Gateway

The virtual tape is comparable to a physical cartridge even if the data resides in a cloud environment. Like physical cassettes, virtual tapes can be empty or contain data, and virtual tapes can be created using the console or using APIs. Each gateway can hold up to 1500 tapes or up to 150TB of data at a time. The size of the virtual tape is configurable and can be between 100GB and 2.5TB.

A VTL "Media Charger" is similar to a physical loader that moves the tapes inside the library, in the slots, or in the tape drives. They supply each VTL with a charger that is directly usable by applications via the iSCSI standard.

Hosting option

In the preceding paragraphs, we have seen that the position of the virtual appliance is always in the corporate data center; in reality, it is possible to position this virtual image even in a cloud environment on EC2, which is very useful in case of disaster recovery. In fact, if your data center goes offline and there are no hosts available, you can activate a gateway on EC2 that continues the alignment operation. Amazon Storage Gateway also provides a pre-packaged AMI image that contains the gateway.

CHAPTER 12

Create An Rds Environment With A High Availability Scalable Database

Amazon RDS is a managed relational database service that allows you to create a DB in the cloud by choosing from six of the most important engines, such as:

Amazon Aurora

MySQL

MariaDB

Oracle

Microsoft SQL

Server

PostgreSQL

You can use the codes, applications, and tools you already use on your database on Amazon RDS.

With the Amazon RDS service, you can manage standard database tasks such as:

Provisioning

Patch application

Backup

Recovery

Error detection

Restoration

2. Simplify the use of replication to increase availability and scalability for production workloads.

3. Perform, thanks to the implementation option, Multi-AZ, synchronously critical workloads with high availability and automated failover integrated from the primary database to a replicated secondary database.

4. Resize, with reading replicas, the resources, and capacity of a single database distribution in case of particularly challenging database reading workloads.

Ease of use Easy

Access to the capabilities of a relational database ready for production thanks to the AWS management console, to the Amazon RDS command-line interface or simple API calls.

Amazon RDS database instances pre-configured according to the parameters and optimal settings for the chosen engine and class.

Starting an instance and connecting with an application in a few minutes

Granular control and database refinement with a DB parameter group

Monitoring and parameters

Amazon CloudWatch parameters for database instances at no additional cost

It displays of the most important operating parameters, such as the use of the calculation capacity, memory, and storage, the I/O activity, and the connections of the instance, all thanks to the AWS Management Console.

Access to over 50 parameters related to CPU, memory, file system, and I/O on disk thanks to Enhanced Monitoring, which provides the. More information

Automatic software patches. Continuous updating of the relational database software that supports the distribution will be with the latest patches.

Performance

Storage for general use (SSD): it is based on SSD, which provides a constant base of 3 IOPS per assigned GB and allows increasing performance up to 3,000 IOPS. This type of storage is suitable for different types of database workloads.

IOPS storage with provisioning (SSD): based on SSD; It provides fast, predictable, and constant I/O performance. It is ideal for I/O intensive transactional database (OLTP) workloads. It Provides up to 30,000 IOPS provisioning per database instance. Actual IOPS may vary depending on the database workload, the type of instance, and the database engine choice.

Scalability

Recalibration of computing and memory resources in just a few clicks, these are simple storage recalibration.

Availability and durability

Automatic backups for point-in-time recovery of the database instance.

Database snapshots, backups initiated manually by the user of the instance saved in Amazon S3, stored until the user explicitly requests to remove it.

Multi-AZ implementations, with multi-zone availability distributions ideal for production database workloads, which, once provisioned, synchronously replicates data on a standby instance located in a separate availability zone.

Automatic: this host the replacement In the event of hardware failure

Security

Data encryption on disk and in transit

Network isolation with Amazon VPC,

Resource-level permissions with AWS Identity and Access Management

Savings

With this, you can calculate prices only based on actual usage

Discounted rates for reserved instances

Interruption and restart

CHAPTER 13

Create A Private Network In The Cloud With Routes And Access Policies

Amazon VPC has the following three features:

High design freedom

Amazon VPC can have one independent IP address range, so you can build an independent network that does not overlap with the Internet and other VPCs, and you can set this IP address range arbitrarily.

In Amazon VPC, you can also divide your network by IP subnet. Therefore, it is possible to design Amazon VPC with a single IP subnet freely, or on the other hand, you can subdivide it according to usage or jurisdiction.

This design flexibility offers the advantage that Amazon VPC and external network IP addresses connection to each other without duplication, and makes it possible to configure access level tiering.

Various external communications are possible by building a network

Amazon VPC itself is completely separated from the external network, but you can communicate with the external network by setting a network gateway. There are three types of network gateways: Internet gateways that enable connection to the Internet, virtual private gateways for VPN communication with your server, and VPC peering connections that connect Amazon VPCs.

By using these network gateways together, communication speed, security, and you can adjust cost according to the application.

Security functions can be used (security group, network ACL)

Amazon VPC has two features that enhance security: security groups and network ACLs.

The security group acts like server firewalls by associating them with AWS resources such as EC2 and RDS. It is possible to use only communication that matches the set rules.

Network ACL is a security function controlled at the IP subnet level. Filtering at a finer level than security groups is possible.

Amazon VPC construction procedure

The procedure to build an Amazon VPC and configure the network is as follows:

Build an Amazon VPC and set up your own DNS using auto-assigned DNS or Amazon Route 53 (AWS recommends designing apps using DNS names, not IP addresses).

IP subnet configuration

Create the necessary IP subnet inside Amazon VPC, and cut out the IP address range and divide the subnet as necessary.

Amazon VPC component placement and route table configuration

Configure an Amazon VPC component for each Amazon VPC and a routing table for each IP subnet. It is necessary to set the component according to the connection destination.

Instance placement

Set the security policy and install the instance.

Name setting

Set the DNS name.

Network to which you can connect VPC

The networks that Amazon VPC can connect to are mainly as follows.

Internal data center (on-premises server)

You can use your own server on the cloud by using virtual VPN communication.

The Internet

You can publish cloud services on the Internet.

Other Amazon VPCs in the same region

If you have Amazon VPCs in the same region, you can connect to other Amazon VPCs. Conversely, if your region is different, be aware that even your own Amazon VPC cannot connect.

Amazon VPC pricing

Amazon VPC is charged depending on the connection to the VPN and the use of the NAT gateway.

NAT gateway usage charges

The meaning of VPN is Virtual private network. It allows companies to expand their central private network practically without geographical limits, creating a "virtual private network," which allows users and peripheral sites (branches) to connect to the "major network" through geographical IP networks leased from telecommunications providers, based on the MPLS protocol (Multiprotocol Label Switching), or public and shared networks such as the Internet and cloud platforms.

Thanks to VPN over the Internet, remote users, or external sites of a company can connect from any part of the world, at any time and with the most disparate devices, to the LAN (Local area network) of their corporate offices, safely and as economically as possible. Within these connections, clients can establish communications with a single computer or with shared technologies with other users such as an application server, a database, a NAS (Network Attached Storage), printers, and so on.

What does tunneling mean?

At the base of the operation of a Virtual Private Network, there is the creation of a tunnel (obviously virtual) within which two or more participants in a virtual private network session can exchange data away from prying eyes. For the creation of this private channel, even if using a shared infrastructure, a tunneling protocol is required. Of these technologies today, there are different ones, but all of them have some aspects in common.

Here's how a VPN works

First of all in the company data center, or in its private cloud (in case you have opted for this solution) a VPN server must be installed, also called Virtual private network Hub or Central Hub, on which all three levels of the security framework of a Virtual Private Network:

- A user authentication system,
- A layer for the management of data encryption methods exchanged between the various network nodes,
- A firewall that controls access to the various network ports

The VPN Hub must also be connected to a router and to one or more switches that allow the assignment of public IP addresses (static or dynamic) to all participants of the VPN (data that must necessarily be present in the header of packets encapsulated in the tunnels).

Therefore, all the devices that users intend to use must be equipped with a VPN client, which can also be:

- A native applet of the device's operating system;

- A software or browser extension downloadable from the site of the VPN service manager;
- A software agent provided with hardware that support the creation of these networks (routers, firewalls, nas, etc.);
- A program developed by a security vendor.

CHAPTER 14

Create A Cloud Storage Environment Through The Amazon S3 Service

Storage as ServiceMove2Cloud transforms the way companies manage and protect their data by providing industry-leading Storage and Cloud Backup solutions that manage, scale, and deliver data protection services transparently and efficiently with high reliability and availability.

We design our on-demand cloud backup services to meet the growing demand for data storage as well as guaranteed recovery without the need for major investments.

Amazon Simple Storage Service (Amazon S3) is an object storage solution with a simple web interface. The service allows you to store any amount of data and retrieve data via the Internet, wherever you are. Amazon S3 delivers 99.999999999% reliability and scalability to more than trillions of sites worldwide.

You can use the Amazon S3 as a repository for large data packets, or a "data lake," for performing analytic tasks, backup and recovery, disaster recovery, and serverless computing. Many applications created and running in the cloud even use S3 as their primary storage.

Amazon's different cloud migration capabilities make it easy to move large amounts of data to and from S3. You can automatically move data written to Amazon S3 to lower-cost cloud storage classes for long-term data storage, such as the standard S3 infrequent access store or Amazon Glacier archive storage.

Benefits of using Amazon simple storage service (Amazon S3)

It enhances Industry-Leading Performance, Scalability, Availability, and Reliability. You can easily increase and reduce storage resources in accordance with fluctuations in requirements, without the need for upfront investment or the cost of acquiring resources. Amazon S3 provides 99.999999999% data reliability (11 nines here) because it automatically creates and stores copies of all objects from S3 in a variety of independent systems. This means that your data is available when you need them and there are no forms of crashes, errors, and threats.

Wide range of cost-effective storage classes

Reduce costs without sacrificing performance by storing data in different S3 storage classes that provide different levels of data access at the right price. You can use S3 storage class analysis to identify the data that you want to migrate to the lower-cost storage class based on access models and configure the S3 lifecycle policy to perform the transfer. You can also store data with changing or unknown access models in the S3 Intelligent-Tiering system, which categorizes objects based on changing access models and automatically reduces costs.

The most comprehensive security, regulatory, and auditing capabilities

Store your data in Amazon S3 and protect it from unauthorized access with encryption and access restriction tools. You can also use the Amazon Macie service to identify sensitive data stored in your S3 baskets and detect suspicious access requests. Amazon S3 complies with regulations such as PCI-DSS, HIPAA / HITECH, FedRAMP, EU Data Protection Directives, and FISMA to help you comply with legal requirements. AWS also supports a variety of auditing capabilities to track requests for access to your resources in S3.

Management tools for precise data control

You can use these tools to classify your data, administer it, and report on it. Using features such as S3 storage class analysis to analyze access models. S3 lifecycle policies help to move objects to storage of less expensive classes. S3 inter-regional replication helps to replicate data to other regions. S3 Object Lock helps to set retention periods for objects and protect them from deletion. S3 Inventory helps to get an idea of their storage objects, their metadata, and encryption. You can also use S3 batch operations to change the properties of objects and perform storage administration operations on billions of objects. Because Amazon S3 works with AWS Lambda, you can log actions,

Non-retrieval data query services for analytics

Analyze big data on your S3 objects (and other AWS datasets) using our services to send data requests without retrieval. Use Amazon Athena to query data in S3 using standard SQL expressions and Amazon Redshift Spectrum to analyze data in AWS repositories and S3 assets. In addition, you can use S3 Select to retrieve the desired datasets for objects instead of entire objects and increase query performance by 400%.

Cloud storage service with better support

Store and protect your data on Amazon S3 with your partner at AWS Partner Network (APN), the largest pool of technology and advisory services providers for cloud services. APN recognizes migration partners who transfer data to Amazon S3, and storage partners who offer S3 integrated storage, backup and recovery, backup, and disaster recovery solutions. You can also purchase the AWS-integrated solution directly in the AWS Marketplace, where you can present more than 250 storage offers.

Amazon S3 offers easy-to-use administration tools that let you organize data and fine-tune access restrictions to meet your business or legal requirements.

CHAPTER 15

Create A Virtual Desktop Environment In The Cloud With Amazon Workspaces

Virtual desktop infrastructure, or VDI, refers to the process of running a user desktop on a virtual machine hosted on a server in the datacenter. It's a powerful form of desktop virtualization because it enables fully customized desktops for every user, with all the security and simplicity of centralized management.

VDI enables customers to simplify management and costs by consolidating and centralizing desktops while providing end-users with mobility and the freedom to access virtual desktops anytime, anywhere, on any device. It is important to understand, however, that VDI is just a form of desktop virtualization.

In this chapter, we would learn the service that AWS offers, which is AWS Workspace. **Your desktop in the cloud.**

Imagine you access your desktop from anywhere and from any device, without investment in CAPEX and Hardware, using everything as a service.

Workspace delivers it all with Windows 7 and 10.

Access the famous AWS console, log in, and search for Workspace. It's quite simple From a Get Started Now.

We have two ways of activation, as if it were a WORKGROUP and the second advance of it creates the directory service within AWS itself. We will choose the simplest way to demonstrate it.

AWS offers several start images from Windows versions, and we will choose the obvious version of Windows 10.

Choose the user, and if you want, you can create one more user. Hit the Launch Workspaces button.

Go to the console and wait for the image creation.

In the process, of course, it already creates the desktop network VPC, and you can create the VPN to put your own Active Directory so you can control the desktops via GPO. This greatly facilitates the process. And the practicalities of AWS with machine snapshots and other AWS services.

Once you create AWS Workspaces, you will be able to access

Go to the URL above "customers.amazonworkspace.com" and choose how to access your VDI. It allows access via Windows, MAC, Linux, Android, and IOS. In addition, it allows web access through browsers.

If it is via the web, register the code or by the applications. You will receive an email to enter your VDI password.

I downloaded the application for Windows and followed the installation sequence

Follow the sequence.

You have received an email to enter the new VDI password, enter the password, and we will access the Desktop.

Wait for access.

Allow Application Access.

You are already accessing the Windows 10 desktop in Amazon Workspace.

See the internal network that AWS offers through VPC.

Below is the sequence for access via ANDROID.

Choose on PlayStore Amazon Workspace

Found it, let's install it. Install the app.

After the installation of the open the application;

Record the code you received for access to the APP.

Enter the code

After receiving the code, it will allow you to enter the username and password of the machine.

Okay, after accessing the username and password, you will have access through a mobile device.

This will give you immense freedom and even access to legacy applications that your company has with Windows 7.

This link gives you a price insight for using Amazon workspace

https: // aws.amazon. com/en/workspaces/pricing/

Remember that usage is a service, and it will transfer your CAPEX to OPEX usage. This gives a great breath of operation management and justifies the use of services without investment in hardware.

It will also bring you again in licensing management, as the operating system licensing is now OPEX related.

For Capex costs, obviously you will reuse your desktop pool and use it as ThinClients with Opensource software or even maintaining Windows operating systems without new investment.

On the other hand, you are investing in low cost thin clients that won't make your Capex high.

CHAPTER 16

Create A Cdn For Content Distribution With Amazon Cloudfront

Cause of Slowness in a website may be due to several reasons. From poor code optimization and images that make up the page like choosing a poor quality web host, to a hosting plan far short of what your site needs. Don't be sad, there is a solution, and the name of this solution is CDN. However, what many do not know is that when using WordPress, it is possible to reduce the slow loading of the site considerably.

This will require the use of a Cache Plugin. After all, what are caches? The cache is a file storage feature of a website. The cache can be on the server or even in your browsers. Have you ever noticed that when you sign in, it takes longer to load than the next time you sign in? This is simply because of your browser stores static files such as images, Html, etc... Therefore, the next time you log into the site, instead of the request being on the server where you host the site, it will be in your own browser, displaying the files that were stored on it faster.

If you want to try it out, go to your browser settings, and clear all cache, history, etc... You'll see that on the next navigation, sites will look slower, and images load slower. This is because, in the first access, the requests are from the server where you hosted the site.

There are features on hosts like varnish cache that already offer a highly effective system for caching your entire site.

Dynamic sites

With the emergence of dynamic sites, that is, sites that connect and store data in databases, the slowness has become greater. Each time you access a page, you can print the displayed content on it through the site's connection to the database and its tables where the content is stored.

For this reason, "static" sites, i.e., without database connection load faster, as they do not need this request.

And to mitigate this, many optimization systems include the cached database optimizing your request.

What is CDN?

Content Delivery Network, or affectionately CDN, is a feature that allows you to approximate the user's request to a closer server. Got confused? I will explain!

When you host a site on a host whether your server is located in the United States, the request from that site to reside far from that server will be greater than the request from those who reside near that server.

Therefore, quite simply, whoever resides closer to where you host your site has a faster request, thus causing a faster site load as well.

What CDN does is to regionalize data storage basically, making it easier for them to access computers from different parts of the planet.

They host certain content on servers spread across multiple parts, thus allowing distribution of contents effectively, regardless of where access is made.

Time and cost savings

CDNs are successful not only because they speed up data transfer between servers and your computer, but also because they are cheaper solutions than maintaining their own structure to do the service, especially if your site's audience is spread across multiple regions of the world.

Amazon CloudFront

Amazon CloudFront is a content delivery network (CDN) offered by Amazon Web Services.

We will integrate your WordPress blog with Amazon CloudFront through the W3 Total Cache Plugin.

The first step is to create an Amazon AWS account. Within the DashBoard, you will have a host of services from Amazon, like CloudFront.

CloudFront1

However, before accessing the service, you must create a user with proper permission to use the feature. What I recommend is that you create a unique username and password for this use. To do this, at the top right of the site, go to Security Credentials.

CloudFront2

When accessing the credential area, on the right side, click on "Users" and later "Create New Users."

CloudFront3

As stated earlier, preferably create a unique user for CDN use.

CloudFront4

In our example, I created a user named "blogcdn." Click on "Create," Then you must click on "Show User Security Credentials" to access the credentials of this created user.

But be careful. Write down these credentials in a safe place and do not share it with anyone if possible.

CloudFront5

Both Access Key ID and Secret Access Key will be used to configure W3 Total Cache, so save them in a text editor, preferably, or download the keys by clicking the "Download Credentials" button in the lower right corner of the screen.

CloudFront6

Now that you have created a user and have the security keys, let's get started? Not! We now need to give CloudFront service permission to the created user.

To do this, click on "Close" in the bottom right corner next to the credentials download button. You will see that the list of created users will appear on the screen.

CloudFront7

Click on the username you created, and on the next screen, click on the "Permissions" tab.

CloudFront8

Now click on the "Attach Policy" button.

CloudFront9

In the next screen, in the search field, you will type the term 'CloudFront.' Note that two versions of the services appear on the screen. One read-only and one for full access. Select both options and click the "Attach Policy" button in the bottom right corner of the screen.

CloudFront10

Ready! From now on, your created user has full access to the CloudFront service.

CloudFront11

Now that we create the user let's create the distribution. Return to the Amazon AWS console home and click on the CloudFront service.

CloudFront12

On the next screen, click "Create Distribution."

CloudFront13

In the next step, click 'Get Started' in the Web tab.

CloudFront14

In the next step, don't be alarmed. Just fill in the distribution name field only, preferably with your site.

The Origin Path field is created automatically from the Origin Domain Name.

Afterward, scroll down to the bottom and click the "Create Distribution" button.

The distribution will be enabled, but will be "In Progress" for about 15 minutes.

CloudFront15

Click on this distribution created by clicking on the link of the column "ID," ie, in our example, and we click on "ER1E47GM7TQMB."

You will enter the distribution settings.

Write down the domain prefix of the created distribution, as we will need it later.

CloudFront16

Opera summary so far!

We created a user, downloaded credentials, and gave that user permission to use the Amazon CloudFront service. Now, let's configure the service integrated with Plugin W3 Total Cache.

First, download the plugin from this link and install it.

The plugin has many interesting settings, but I recommend that you configure it very carefully, as any incorrect configuration can cause serious problems on your site.

After installing the plugin, on the right side, click on "Performance" and then "General Settings."

CloudFront12

In the "Page Cache" settings, check "Enable."

CloudFront14

Scroll down further and go to "Brose cache." Enable the option.

CloudFront15

Just below "Browse Cache," we will enable the CDN service for the plugin and select the CloudFront service.

CloudFront16

But beware! You'll need a lot of attention at this time. In "CDN Type," choose "Amazon CloudFront" from "Origin Pull/mirror," as shown below.

CloudFront17

After enabling CDN and choosing the type, save the settings by clicking "Save all settings."

Now go back to the "Performance" item in the side menu and go to the "CDN" item.

CloudFront13

A little below, under "configuration," we will start integrating with the distribution we created on Amazon CloudFront. This is where the game will really begin: p

CloudFront18_2

Enter the Access Key ID you copied or saved from Amazon.

Enter Secret Key

Origin will appear automatically after setting up CDN here, so as soon as you save the settings, your website address will appear there.

In this field, you will have to enter the domain prefix of this created distribution. We saw this during the creation of the distribution, as shown below:

CloudFront24

PS: Enter only the prefix.

5. You can create on your host a CNAME annotation for a subdomain, i.e., something like cdn.yoursite.com or static.yourite.com. To do this, set up this pointing or redirecting directly to your host or open a ticket for your host to make this setting. The pointing should be not only for the domain prefix of the distribution but for all of it, as shown below:

d1ya6xvwacpff8.cloudfront.net> cdn.yoursite.com

This way, the site images, for example, will open this way: http: // cdn.yoursite. com/wp-content/uploads/2016/01/logo1.png instead of http: // d1ya6xvwacpff8. cloudfront.net/wp-content/uploads/2016/01/logo1.png.

Once you've done that, click save settings, open your site, and open the images in a new window to make sure it's already configured with Amazon CloudFront CDN.

This can dramatically reduce bandwidth costs, act as a backup, and help speed up your site.

Amazon S3 is a storage solution, and many Amazon products are part of Amazon Web Services. They use this typically for large sites that need additional backups or are serving large files (downloads, software, videos, games, audio files, PDFs, etc.). Amazon has a proven record of accomplishment of being very reliable and, because of its massive infrastructure, is able to offer very low storage costs. Some of S3's clients include Netflix, Airbnb, SmugMug, NASDAQ, etc.

WordPress Amazon S3

Because Amazon S3 deals entirely with mass storage, you can almost guarantee that the price will be lower than your WordPress host will. Downloading media to AWS can be a great way to save money, and it's free for your first year (up to 5 GB of storage). In addition, since the answer to the requests for your media are directly from Amazon, this puts fewer loads on your WordPress site, which means faster load times.

Conclusion

Cloud Computing is a model that enables, in an omnipresent, convenient, and on-demand way, the access, via the network, to a shared pool.

In this book, we have briefly presented the capabilities of Amazon cloud computing service; despite the young age cloud computing, these systems are rapidly gaining considerable market shares, although doubts persist in more than one doubt about the actual opportunity to bring everything to the cloud. You can elastically assign and release rapid elasticity resources in some cases, automatically to rapidly scale outwards and inwards in relation to demand. For users, the resources available for assignment often seem unlimited and you can assign in any quantity and at any time

In the course of this book, the services offered by Amazon were introduced, both because of the popularity it enjoys and because it is currently one of the most matures offers on the market in this area. As discussed, capabilities make it suitable for hosting arbitrary load servers at relatively low prices. This makes it attractive for multiple uses, from the Web server to scientific computing. Its advanced yet simple management interface allows its users to a vast and not necessarily technical public.

During its technological maturation process, in particular, relating to the definition of open standards, cloud computing is going to establish itself substantially as the main element in the management of low/medium load servers, replacing the various hosting/housing managers that offer VPS solutions without any benefit. Similarly, the possibility of using high-performance parallel computing systems paying only for execution times could represent a viable alternative for small scientific computing centers in the future. As for critical systems and/or high load/reliability systems, there are still several unknowns relating to the economic and technological convenience of transferring all of their IT systems to the "cloud."

Don't miss out!

Visit the website below and you can sign up to receive emails whenever Theo H. King publishes a new book. There's no charge and no obligation.

https://books2read.com/r/B-A-TRDV-GIIBC

BOOKS 2 READ

Connecting independent readers to independent writers.